THE AMERICAN DREAM

THE AMERICAN DREAM

FINANCIAL TIPS FOR NEWLY WEDS

CODY ZIEMER

To order additional copies of this book, contact:
Xlibris Corporation
1-888-795-4274
www.Xlibris.com
Orders@Xlibris.com
66625

CONTENTS

The American Dream. The elusive utopia that is just outside of our grasps. Americans throughout these fifty states have a unique version of their American Dream. Some plan to own a business, some plan to be a rock star, some plan to work up the corporate ladder. While these goals are vastly different, they all have one common element for the dreamer to achieve them: hard work. Fortunately for many Americans, hard work is not a problem. We are a society that values hard work because we know that majority of the time, hard work pays off. There are those few instances when you meet the perfect storm, and no matter how hard you try, it just does not work, but those scenarios are few and far between. So if we are willing to put the work in, we will find that little bit of luck that propels us toward our dreams.

Unfortunately, we do not transfer these same principles into our finances. While working as a financial advisor, there was one question that I had to ask: "How do you plan to fund your retirement?" The answers varied, especially by age. The younger people that had little to no financial background just assumed by the time they were "old," they would have a great job and the ability to save money. Then I would meet with these "old" people that had the same idea when they were young. Invariably they were wrong. Now they are looking at retirement and beginning to realize that at best it will be several years past sixty-five before they could retire, and even then they would be a greeter at Wal-Mart. (I'm not saying that all greeters at Wal-Mart failed to plan for retirement; it's just a loosely used stereotype.)

It was refreshing to meet the young people that actually understood financial matters. These were the people that began maxing out their 401(k)'s and started contributing to Roth IRAs (the second-best financial decision you could ever make, but more on that later). These were the people that made my job easy. I did not have to sell them on the idea that they needed to save. Instead, I just needed to find them the best possible vehicle to begin accumulating money.

There was also one other group that I truly enjoyed working with: the people in their late to midforties that had understood the value of saving at a young age. These people had put themselves in a great position for the future. I remember meeting with one individual whose biggest problem was that he had saved more than he had planned on, so he was trying to decide how early he wanted to retire. Oh that we all had that problem right? While I might have been the expert on what tax-saving strategy to use, it was these people that I went to for advice. People that have financial stability have better marriages, less stress, and more fulfilled lives. These are the people that I want to give me advice, and from my introduction, I bet you can guess what that advice was—yes, hard work and discipline.

This book is specific for young people. I want you to read this when you still have a chance to direct your financial future. Hopefully, this book can help you avoid some huge mistakes in life and, more importantly, help you take advantage of opportunities that arise. So for the next few chapters, I am giving you the wisdom that I have gleaned both from my experience and from the experience of other people that have built a solid financial foundation.

Goals

"If one does not know to which port one is sailing, no wind is favorable." Lucius Annaeus Seneca, the Roman philosopher, once said these words to illustrate the importance of goals in our life. If we do not have a clear, distinct direction of where we are going, then we will never get there. We tend to apply this to many aspects in our life, but on many occasions, I meet people that do not transfer it to their personal finances. Without financial goals, we will never know what strategies are favorable because there is no way to monitor them. We are the proverbial ship tossed at sea with no direction. All throughout ancient times, nautical travel has been extremely dangerous. Once a ship gets away from the dock and out in the ocean, there are little to no landmarks for them to use. Sailors found crude ways to establish direction through timing logs, the stars, and the sun. Unfortunately, these methods resulted in the deaths of thousands of sailors that had become lost at sea.

In the seventeen hundreds, Great Britain decided to find a way to accurately decide a ship's longitude while on the ocean. Queen Anne offered twenty thousand pounds to anyone that could find a suitable way to accurately determine longitude. The race came down to clockmakers and astronomers, with John Harrison, the clockmaker, finally winning out. He found a clock that could stay accurate even when sailors exposed it to the extreme weather conditions of the sea. This clock allowed the sailors to determine their longitude and therefore accurately map a course to their destination.

You may be wondering what ships and clocks have to do with you reaching your financial goals. Well, it is the best example I could find that shows the importance of setting goals. First off, you have to set a goal as to where you are going financially. You need one-, three-, five-, ten-, twenty-, and thirty-year goals. A very good question to keep in mind is, "What three things need to happen by the end of that time period for you to feel satisfied?" For most people, their ultimate goal is to retire early. So that would be the thirty-year goal for a twenty-five-year-old couple. Then all of the other goals on their list need to ultimately lead to their final goal. For example, my thirty-year goal is to be retired and debt free. So my three-year goal is to have my vehicles and all student loans paid off. My five-year goal is to have a home purchased and $20,000 set aside for retirement, my ten-year goal is to have $100,000 set aside for retirement, and my twenty-year goal is to have my home paid for and $200,000 set aside for retirement. All of these goals are working toward my ultimate goal. So if you look back to the nautical reference, the main goal is to get to the dock. These short-term goals are the clocks that allowed the sailors to determine whether they were on course or not.

Goals, and especially big goals, are important in all aspects of your life. One time I was at the gym working out and I met this older gentleman there. As we began talking, he asked me what my goal was for the bench press. I thought about it and told him I really did not have a goal. It was more of a stress relief to come in and put some weight on a bar and push. His response was that in everything that you find important enough to do in your life, you need to set goals. This is true; I held fitness as being important, so I had an overall goal of being physically fit. However, I had not made the smaller goals with the individual lifts and workouts that would allow me to obtain the major goal.

These minor or short-term goals allow us to hold ourselves accountable. We can see what areas we are excelling in and what areas we are sinning. I use this word not in a religious sense, but it was also an old archery term that meant to miss the mark. An archer uses a target to show where his arrows are hitting. He then can adjust his aim to zero in on the bull's-eye. The same holds true in our financial situations. If we are off a little on our three-year goal, we are going to be off a little more on our five-year goal, until finally we are not even close to our thirty-year goal. We must use these short-term goals to monitor our progress and make changes accordingly. Most importantly, do not be afraid to dream big. Big goals will push you outside of your comfort zone and push you to reach your full capacity. Just be smart about it.

You might have noticed that I left out the one-year goal. That's because I will make this goal for you. The one-year goal for every young person or couple is *financial stability*. This is the foundation that will allow you to obtain all the lofty goals that you set for yourself. The next chapter explains financial stability in detail.

Financial Stability

I define financial stability as the ability to maintain the things you value the most, in all scenarios except a severe economic depression. For this definition, I want to say you can maintain them in any scenario, but we all know there are circumstances beyond our control. So let us take a look at what these things might be that we value so highly. Some important things for me are my family and the ability to support them, my health, my home, and a vehicle simply because I need it for transportation. As a financial advisor, I found a pyramid illustrates the hierarchy of the financially sound individuals (couple); here is the bottom portion that shows financial stability.

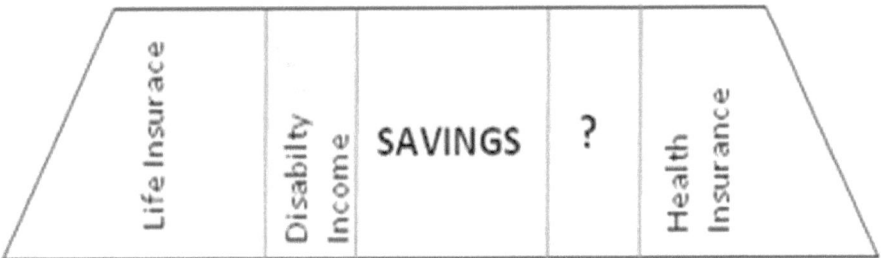

SAVINGS

As you can see, the cornerstone to this pyramid is savings. A savings account is the most important part of financial stability. You should have at least three months of income sitting in a very liquid account. A liquid account is one that is easily accessible (i.e., checking account, savings account). This is your emergency money that will keep you out of debt.

DEBT

Your main concern with this account is not to earn interest but rather to avoid *credit card* debt. I want to start off by explaining credit card debt. It is all unnecessary or unplanned purchases. If you are at the mall and you see a new designer purse that you just have to have to match those ladies' shoes, the easiest way to purchase it is with a VISA. That way, you do not take the hit right now and you can spread it out over a few years at $20 a month. This is the worst possible thing you can do. Purchasing things this way ends up costing you hundreds, if not thousands, more than the original price. Debt that you create with your VISA is not the only type of credit card debt I am talking about. We have all heard the commercial that today is the great time to take a second mortgage on your house and take that trip to Disneyland you have always dreamed about. Quite frankly, this is a horrible idea and here is why. Suppose you take out a $20,000 second mortgage to take a trip to Disneyland and buy that boat you want. If you take a conventional thirty-year loan at 8%, by the time you pay off the loan, you will have paid an additional $32,800 in interest. That is more than you originally borrowed. So in reality, your dream vacation and boat cost you $52,800! Having a savings account with three months' worth of income in it would allow you take the vacation and maybe even buy the boat and save you $32,800. This example is based upon an 8% interest rate. An 8% interest rate is about normal for most loans for an individual with good credit. The interest rate changes due to economic situations, but that is about normal for a loan. Credit cards are almost always higher since they can go all the way up into the 20% interest rates. This makes a huge difference when it comes to paying off the loan. If the same thirty-year loan above had an interest rate of 20%, you would end up paying out $120,500 instead of the $52,800. The interest rate means a lot, so pay attention to the rates when you are looking at a loan. Another problem with credit cards is that if your credit history changes, credit card companies have the right to raise your interest rate to the highest level possible. The most common reason for this is a person misses a credit card payment; once this happens, that credit card, plus all the other credit cards you have, can raise their interest rates. So paying your bills on time can literally save you thousands of dollars.

All my examples so far have been on the unnecessary side of the argument. Now let us look at the unplanned side. Assume that you lose your job. In the late 1990s, this was not a problem, you lose your job, great—you can probably find a better one within a few weeks. However, that was not the case in late 2008 into 2009. The job market severely contracted, leaving hundreds of thousands without jobs. Here, that three-month cushion would be ideal. Given time, the economy will recover; however, you need to be able to support yourself and your family through that time. If you do not have that cushion, then you must use debt. So assuming you put $1,000 a month on credit cards for a three-month period, you now have a $3,000 credit card balance and an average interest rate of 12%. If you can find $100 a month to pay toward the balance, it will take you three years and cost you $587 in interest. If you can only pay $66 a month, it will take you five years and cost $1,000 in interest. Plus your savings is completely depleted, and you must begin putting money away to build it back up. With a savings account established, you can ride through this period without taking on debt.

Another example of unplanned credit card debt when your savings account can be extremely vital is emergencies. We never know what will happen tomorrow. Your car could break down, you could have an accident, you could see a 1967 Mustang Fastback for sale—there are many things that could happen almost daily that require significant amounts of our income. If you apply the same scenario as above with $3,000 on credit at 12% interest, you can see how using the money in savings and then repaying it will save you 20-30% of that amount you originally borrowed. Having an emergency savings account gives you the best opportunity to obtain financial stability.

LEVERAGED AND NECESSARY DEBT

So far, you may believe that I think debt is the evil. You are right. Debt is the primary reason most people do not reach their financial goals. However, I do not think debt is always a bad thing; it just has to be used correctly. My dad always told me a saying that he picked up from somewhere: "Debt is a beautiful slave, and a terrible master." This is the truth. So how can we use debt as our slave? Well, the answer is to leverage it. Franco Modigliani and Merton Miller came up with some interesting findings about how to use debt. To understand this, we need to look at Accounting 101. A company's balance sheet is made up of three parts: assets, liabilities, and equity. To simplify it, assets are things that a business owns, such as a building, machinery, trucks, etc. Liabilities are the debt that company takes on to purchase these assets. Equity is the money that the owners have put in to buy these assets. So if you look at the value of all the assets that a company owns, you will find that the total liabilities and equity added together equals the same amount.

What Modigliani and Miller did in one of their studies is show that equity is really expensive when the company is doing well. A simple way to understand this is to think about starting your own business. You decide that you will need $50,000 to do so, so you call your rich uncle and tell him your business idea. He thinks it is a great idea and agrees to give you the money, but he wants to own 50% of the business. This money that he gives you is equity. As a 50% owner, he receives 50% of all profits. So if the company makes $100,000, he gets $50,000; but if the company makes $1,000,000, he is now entitled to $500,000. The better the business does, the more money you have to pay your uncle. If you would have gone to the bank and borrowed the money, you will have retained 100% ownership. So you borrow $50,000 with a 10% payment for five years, and then the bank will want you to pay back the whole $50,000. It does not matter how the business does; you are only required to pay $5,000 a year. If you make a $1,000,000, you only have to pay $5,000 a year.

So how does this help you in your everyday life? Well, using debt for investments is a good idea. Here, I am not promoting maxing out your credit cards and putting the money in the stock market. I am talking about investing in a home or a piece of land or something of that nature. Think about purchasing a home. The majority of us cannot graduate college and then go pay cash for a home. You will probably have to use debt. Home prices have risen steadily over the last thirty years. At one point it seemed to be the only sure investment. While there have been downturns in the housing markets, homes have retained their value very well overall.

Investing in a home is a good idea for a young person or couple. If you did not want to use debt to pay for the home, you would have to save enough money to make the purchase. To do so, you would probably have to live with your parents and put away at least $1,500 a month for nine years to have enough to purchase an average home. The bad part is that homes appreciate in value over time. If you do not believe this, ask your parents how much homes were in the 1970s and compare that to today. If you continue to save and save to buy a home, the price for the home will go up each year. (I know there are years that the price declines, but overall prices have gone up.) Had you used debt to purchase the home, you could have bought the house at $200,000 and watched it appreciate at 3% a year over those nine years, and you now have $61,000 in price appreciation plus whatever you have been able to pay on the loan. It does not matter how much the house appreciates—you still have a set payment that does not increase. While the debt will cost you more in the long run, you can make up for this with price appreciation, plus not living with your parents for an additional nine years has to count for something.

HEALTH INSURANCE

The next major element on the pyramid base is health insurance. This is extremely important for the same reason as the emergency savings account; you just never know what will happen. A major medical emergency could deplete all your assets and leave you with substantial debt. Medical costs have risen exponentially, and the trend seems to be that they will continue to rise. This is why health insurance is so important. Without it, you are completely vulnerable to the escalating costs.

In addition to the protection, health insurance is cheaper for healthy young individuals. (Especially males, since women are in their childbearing years). So in some cases, as you get older with more medical problems, it becomes extremely expensive, to almost impossible, to get health insurance. Fortunately, if you are working, you can receive group coverage with no underwriting.

Another concern is, do you purchase individual health insurance, or do you take advantage of the group insurance through your employer? The answer really varies by individual, but new COBRA laws have made the two choices almost identical. If you have a serious medical condition and you are laid off, you can keep the insurance through your old employer for several months until you find other work, so you are not just left out completely uninsured.

LIFE INSURANCE AND DISABILITY INCOME

I combine these two elements for the simple reason that I do not think they are important until you have a family. Disability income is usually only a concern for young people if they are highly paid professionals such as doctors. Doctors usually have substantial student loans when they graduate and begin practicing medicine. This debt is not a real problem since they have a relatively high income when they start out. However, if the doctor is a surgeon and he injures his hands, his career is over and he still has these student loans. Disability income would compensate for the loss of income and allow him to maintain the lifestyle that he worked for.

For almost all other cases, disability income is not a priority until you have a family to support. Then disability becomes a concern, and I can personally attest to this. My father was the primary breadwinner in our home. At forty-five years old, he was severely injured on the job and could never work again; because we did not have disability income, our whole lifestyle was changed. From that time forward, my mom became the primary breadwinner. Thankfully, the United States government has social programs to assist with disabilities; however, it is nowhere near the level of income that he made working.

Life insurance is used to replace income from a spouse's death. Again you do not need life insurance until you have a family. When I would meet with clients to determine how much life insurance they needed, we figured out their income, how much of that income the family would need to maintain their lifestyle, total debt, and future goals. Most young couples that just got married do not have the goal of paying off their home and sending their kids to college for a very good reason—they do not have a home or kids yet. Your financial goals when you are recently married are completely different from those you will have five years later. As we talked about earlier, your financial goals now are simple. You may want to include these big long-term goals of sending your kids to college, establishing a legacy, and making significant contributions to your charity of choice, but they are not your primary focus right now. You must build a solid financial foundation before you can move on to these next goals. Life insurance is there to make sure the ones you love obtain these big long-term goals for you if you are not around to do so.

TERM INSURANCE VERSUS PERMANENT INSURANCE

These are the two major types of insurance: term and permanent. Term insurance is rented for a set time period: ten, twenty, or thirty years. The lower the amount of years and the healthier you are, the cheaper your insurance premiums. Permanent is insurance for the rest of your life. You have a set monthly premium you pay until you die. If you are comparing prices, term insurance is significantly cheaper than permanent because insurance companies usually only pay out 2-4% of term insurance policies. Permanent, on the other hand, is always paid out as long as the insured makes the premiums. We all will die someday.

Another reason that the permanent insurance is more expensive is the cash value buildup in the policy. In many cases, the cost of insurance for the contract is relatively low, and then you pay in a little extra money that builds up just like a savings account. Depending on the policy, you can usually invest this money in certain funds within the policy to maximize your return. Make sure you discuss the investment strategy with your insurance representative because the insurance company may require certain asset allocations (we will talk about this in the investment chapter in great detail) to guarantee the contract will be paid. Term insurance does not have this cash buildup. It is strictly the cost of insurance. So any time you meet with an insurance representative, he or she will want to sell you permanent life insurance. Depending on how ethical he or she is will determine if they want to sell it to you because they think it is a good fit or if he or she wants to make more money on the sale. Permanent life insurance pays the representative *a lot* better than term life insurance.

So if you know that the representative wants to sell you permanent life insurance and you meet with him or her, how do you know if it is the best fit for you? Fortunately for a young couple, this is relatively easy. If you are not maxing out the contribution to your Roth IRAs for both spouses, then there is a 99% chance you do not need permanent life insurance. Tax laws in the United States have several loopholes in them, one of which is life insurance. Right now, the proceeds from a life insurance policy are not taxable in most cases. There are some weird third-party cases where the proceeds become a gift, but that is usually a mistake on the representative's side. So if you are the policy owner or the beneficiary, any proceeds from the policy are tax free. Which means you can take loans against this cash value building up in your policy, tax free. This sounds like the best plan in the world. I get to put money in an account, let it build up with interest, and then pull my money plus the interest I earned and not pay taxes. However, this is where the Roth IRA comes into play. The Roth IRA has almost the same tax laws; you pay taxes on your income and then put the extra money into a Roth IRA. You invest this money, and then when you are fifty-nine and a half, you can pull this money out tax free. There are also loopholes in the tax law that allows you to begin pulling your principal out sooner.

Now that you know the tax laws for both the permanent life insurance and the Roth IRA are identical, we will look at the fee structure of the two. A Roth IRA is nothing more than an account you set up. You have complete liberty to invest this money in anything from a money market account to small cap stocks. Your fees in this account are strictly limited to your transactions and the cost of any mutual funds in your portfolio (again we will go into detail about all this in the investment chapter, so right now just trust me). However, with permanent life insurance, you must pay all the investment costs that you get in a Roth IRA plus the cost of insurance in your policy. These extra fees will destroy your long-term gains. Assuming you and your spouse contribute the maximum of $5,000 a year for the next twenty years into a Roth IRA and make a 9% interest rate while paying a 1% investment fee, you will have $409,000 at the end. If you make the same contributions into a permanent life insurance policy with the same funds and costs, plus the 1% cost of insurance, you will have $366,000 at the end of the twenty-year period. That extra 1% cost of insurance equals $43,000 dollars.

For the vast majority of young couples, term life insurance makes more sense. It is substantially cheaper and gives the couple more money to contribute to a far superior investment vehicle: the Roth IRA.

THE LAST BUILDING BLOCK

The final building block has to be defined by the individual. Personally for me, it is tithing. I hold tithing as a very important conviction in my life, and I believe that it is essential to the rest of my goals and dreams. You need to find what that is for you. For some people, it is planning for long-term care insurance, some it is charitable giving, others do not find anything to put here, so they add it to the savings. That is up to you, and I cannot and will not tell you what your values should be.

STABILITY

Once you have these components in place, you are in better financial shape than 80% of the world. It does not matter what happens—you are prepared to make it through. You have a strong base that will allow you to reach your big dreams and your big goals.

If I look out the window in my office, I see an old cottonwood tree on the edge of a little embankment. Some of the neighborhood kids built a fort in it with a rope swing. They tied plastic strips together to make a rope. They tied it to the branches and use it to swing into the fort. I sat there watching them one day and realized that the rope was the only way for them to get into the fort, unless they walked all the way around the embankment and climbed halfway up the tree. So for all intents and purposes, that rope swing was the only way for them to go into the fort. As time went by, that plastic rope broke, and now there is a great fort, but nobody plays there anymore. The rope was not stable enough to give them access to the fort. The same is true for your financial future. If you do not get this portion right, you might have big dreams, but you will not have access to them. So now that you know what elements you need in place to obtain your dreams, I will show you the magic tool that will make it possible: the budget.

Budgeting

Developing a budget is the single best financial decision you will ever make. Unfortunately, this is where the hard work begins. To create a budget, you must be disciplined. *Discipline* is such a horrible word; it brings back horrible memories from our childhood of being grounded from the TV, being grounded from our friends, not being able to go out on Friday night, and, for some of us, spankings. Yet discipline is a very important part of our life. So maybe our parents were trying to teach us something and were not just reincarnations of medieval torture specialists. The beautiful thing about a budget is that it shows us exactly what areas in our life we need to show more discipline in. Let's look at an example of a budget for a fictional couple, John and Mildred. Between the two, they make $5,000 a month and live in a normal neighborhood. Right now we will ignore taxes just to make the example easier. They kept the receipts for the last three months and sat down to make their budget. Here is what they found:

2008 Budget

	January	February	March
Income	$ 5,000	$ 5,000	$ 5,000
Expenses			
Rent	1,500	1,500	1,500
Utilities	300	300	300
Food	150	150	150
Car payments	600	600	600
Car insurance	200	200	200
Health insurance	350	350	350
Gas	250	250	250
Cell phone	150	150	150

Internet and cable	150	150	150
Health club	50	50	50
Entertainment	1,000	1,000	1,000
401(k)	300	300	300
Total leftover for Savings	$ -	$ -	$ -

Fortunately for us, they spend the exact same amount every month on everything. What a coincidence. They also lumped clothing, eating out, partying, credit card bills, etc., into entertainment. When we look at the budget, there are a few things that speak very highly for this couple's financial knowledge. One is the rent; it is only 30% of their monthly take home. We will talk about why this is good later on in the debt section. Another is the car payments—they did not go all out on extravagant vehicles, and lastly is the fact that they are contributing to a 401(k) plan. However, there are some problems. They are spending everything they have left over on entertainment, 20% of their budget.

The biggest problem with this budget is the order. If you look, the 401(k) and savings are the last two items on the budget. For many of us, that is exactly how our budget works. Retirement is so far away that it is hard to cut back on entertainment to put money away for it. Savings is nice, but there are so many other things I would like to do with this money, and they are having a great sale at Nordstrom. We have all been there, we know what we should do, but we never do it. This is where discipline comes in to play. If we develop the budget correctly, then we will be able to obtain our goals.

If John and Mildred have put their savings as the leftover parts of their budget, then I would bet money that they do not have three months of income in savings. So they are already missing the cornerstone of their financial pyramid.

To avoid falling into the same trap as John and Mildred, you must remember the basic concept of paying yourself first. That is the "magic" behind a budget. It forces you to take money out for savings before you get to the entertainment section. The first year is always the hardest because you need to put more money away to build up the emergency savings fund. If you put away 20% for savings, you will have three months of income in the bank in fifteen months. So many times, we look at savings as an afterthought when it should be a main priority. When you are in the Bass Pro Shop and looking at the boats, make sure you can make the payment after you put money in savings, not instead of putting money in savings. So let us make some changes to this budget for John and Mildred.

2008 Budget Revised

	January	February	March
Income	$ 5,000	$ 5,000	$ 5,000
Expenses			
Savings	1,000	1,000	1,000
Rent	1,500	1,500	1,500
Life Insurance	50	50	50
Utilities	300	300	300
Food	150	150	150
Car payments	600	600	600
Car insurance	200	200	200
Health Insurance	350	350	350
Gas	250	250	250
Cell Phone	150	150	150
Internet and Cable	150	150	150
Health Club	50	50	50
Total Leftover for Entertainment	$ 250.00	$ 250.00	$ 250.00

As you can see, the increased savings requires a drastic decrease in entertainment spending. You may have also noticed that I took out their contributions to their 401(k). If I have to choose between the emergency savings and the 401(k), I will go for the emergency savings. Once they have the savings built up, they need to start the 401(k) distributions again. Ideally, they could find something else to cut. In addition to the savings, I also added in life insurance. A term life insurance policy for a healthy young couple is not expensive at all and should be easy to squeeze into a budget. So now John and Mildred have the three most important cornerstones. Again disability income insurance is somewhat of a personal preference. It is a good benefit to have, but you need to decide if that benefit is greater than the cost. For all of my examples, I will exclude it.

OK, after the fifteen months, John and Mildred have their emergency savings account in place. Now they can cut back on their savings and build a budget that is a little easier to live on. To build up the savings, the couple needed to save 20% of their income; now we can drop that to 10% and begin saving for retirement. Here is the new modified budget.

y

20

2009 Budget

	April	May	June
Income	$ 5,000	$ 5,000	$ 5,000
Expenses			
Savings	250	250	250
401(k)	150	150	150
Roth IRA	100	100	100
Rent	1,500	1,500	1,500
Life insurance	50	50	50
Utilities	300	300	300
Food	150	150	150
Car payments	600	600	600
Car insurance	200	200	200
Health insurance	350	350	350
Gas	250	250	250
Cell phone	150	150	150
Internet and cable	150	150	150
Health club	50	50	50
Total leftover for Entertainment	$ 750.00	$ 750.00	$ 750.00

The couple will continue to contribute to the savings at 5% of their income. This is the money they use instead of a credit card. So if they need tires or John breaks a finger trying to be Kobe Bryant on the basketball court, they have money put away to take care of it without taking on any debt. If they find they do not have anything that comes up that month, then great, they add more money to the savings, and we already talked about why more money in savings is a good thing. The other 5% goes toward retirement accounts. Here I used two accounts: one is the 401(k) plan through their work and the other is the Roth IRA. The reason for this is the Roth IRA is the superior savings plan. However, the 401(k) gives the couple a tax deduction, plus most companies will match your contributions to your 401(k) up to 3% of your income. For the budget, I allowed 3% to go to the 401(k) so that they could maximize the amount the company will contribute, and the rest goes to the Roth IRA. In the next chapter we will discuss this topic in much more detail, so do not try to figure this out if it is giving you problems. One other sidebar, I would not carry more than six months of income in your emergency savings account. If you are charmed and nothing ever bad happens to you, then you should have six months of income in your emergency savings in five years. That is plenty, and from then on, I would use that 5% for retirement savings.

Another difference in the new budget from the old one is that their money left over for entertainment tripled. This gives the couple the ability to go back to some of the things they enjoy or apply this extra 10% of income toward other goals. In the goals section, I mentioned that my three-year goal was to have my vehicles paid off. It is conceivable that if I took half of that extra 10% and applied it to my car payments, I could achieve this by the end of three years. So let us take a look at one more budget at the three-year mark. For this budget, I made one more assumption, that somewhere in that three-year period, John and Mildred got a raise of $500 a month between the two.

2011 Budget Revised

	January	February	March
Income	$ 5,500	$ 5,500	$ 5,500
Expenses			
Savings	275	275	275
401(k)	165	165	165
Roth IRA	110	110	110
Rent	1,500	1,500	1,500
Life insurance	50	50	50
Utilities	300	300	300
Food	150	150	150
Car payments	—	—	—
Car insurance	200	200	200
Health insurance	350	350	350
Gas	250	250	250
Cell phone	150	150	150
Internet and cable	150	150	150
Health club	50	50	50
Total leftover for Entertainment	$ 1,800.00	$ 1,800.00	$ 1,800.00

If John and Mildred decided to cut back on entertainment and paid off the cars, they now have an extra $1,800 a month. This is over and above the 10% they are saving.

They have at least $15,000 dollars in the bank, plus almost double the amount for entertainment that they had just three years ago!

Now is when they must look at their goals. They have reached the three-year period and need to look at what they need to accomplish in the next two years to obtain their five-year goal. Mine was to purchase a home and have $20,000 set aside for retirement. So look at the retirement first. If the market has performed at 8% (its historical average), then I will have $15,500 at my five-year goal. So it looks like I need to begin increasing what I pay into my Roth IRA. If we do a simple present value calculation, we see that we need another $175 to go to the Roth IRA. Even with the additional Roth IRA contributions, the couple has 30% of their income open for entertainment. Originally, we said that this was too much, and I still believe so. Here is where the second goal comes into play. John and Mildred have an extra $900 over their allotted entertainment money from the previous two years. If they raise their entertainment budget back up to $1,000 a month where they started originally, they will still have $650 left over. This money can go into a separate savings account for future purchases, such as the house. If they put this money in a higher-yielding money market account or a bond account, they could gain around a 3% return and still have a high degree of liquidity with the money. This would give them $22,000 at the five-year mark to purchase a home. With first-time home buyer programs, this amount should be sufficient for them to purchase a home. So here comes year 5 and they can mark off both goals and turn toward the ten-year goals.

In this last section, we made a generic budget that showed how a couple can get themselves on the way to obtaining their financial goals in three years. The first fifteen months takes a lot of discipline, but it is vital to building financial stability. Once that foundation is in place, you can begin to enjoy things more and watch your wealth begin to accumulate. The budget has to change over time; in fact, your budget might change every three months or so. However, make sure you keep your focus on your goals, especially through the first fifteen-month period.

I would recommend doing all your budgets in Microsoft Excel. The program makes budgeting very simple because it makes adding and subtracting easy. Your budget is your ideal spending pattern; you want to hold on to it as closely as possible, but we all understand that other things happen and life changes. Some of these changes can be planned out in advance, however. Take, for instance, John's and Mildred's cars. The cars are at least three years old but paid off. If they think that they will need a new car within the next four years, they should start planning for that now. The budget is the perfect place to begin. Before, we know that their car payments were $600 a month for presumably five years. Well, if they begin planning for that car payment two years in advance, it could save them a tremendous amount of money. Let us assume they cannot find $600 a month in their budget but they can find $400. So for the two years up to the purchase date, they put away $400 in a money market account earning 3%. At the end of the two years, they will have $9,800 in the bank for their future purchase. When John goes to the car lot, he falls in love with a $30,000 BMW 330i and trades in his old car for $2,000. He then puts the $9,800 down on the car and takes a loan out for $18,200. With a 5% interest rate, his payments will be $417 a month for only four years.

Now if we go back and look at what the payments would be without the down payment, we will see the savings. If they would have taken a loan out for the whole $28,000, they will pay $31,700 ($528 a month for sixty months). With the down payment, they will pay a total of $29,600 and save themselves $2,100 or 7% of the total loan. If John and Mildred wanted to be really frugal, they would begin making the $400 payments back to their savings as soon as they could. This is the concept of self-lending. You loan yourself the money, but then you have to be disciplined enough to pay it back. Quite frankly, almost nobody is disciplined enough to pay this back.

There is another benefit to saving before a purchase. If John would have known when he began saving that he wanted a BMW 330i, then he could figure out the payment for it. If you recall, the payment was $528 for five years. So John and Mildred begin taking $528 a month out of their entertainment money and put it away. After six months, they will have a very good idea of what life will be like with that payment. John may decide that it is too much of a sacrifice and he will find a car that is cheaper. Fortunately, they did not just waste $3,000 in car payments to find that out. He still has that money sitting in a bank account. By using a budget to plan ahead, you can save yourself from making costly mistakes.

As I am sure you have already figured out, discipline is the key to financial stability and wealth building. An undisciplined person will never be wealthy unless they have an unlimited supply of cash. You must learn to discipline yourself if you want to succeed at anything. Michael Jordan was not just good at basketball. He had some natural talent, but it was not even good enough for him to make his high school basketball team at one point. Through discipline and hard work, he achieved his goals. The same is true for you. If you cannot develop a passion that connects your goals to why you are saving a significant amount of your income, then you will probably never develop the discipline required to make it work. You have to link your actions with your goals. If all you can see is that you have to give up your country club membership and 72 oz. Jose Cuervo Gold margaritas for 24 oz. generic ones, then you will never be able to make it work. You might as well take this book back and see if you can get your money back. However, if you can see that giving up these things now will mean in a few years you can live a much more extravagant lifestyle without the heavy burden of debt, then keep on plugging away at this book. You are the type of person that can and will reach your financial goals.

In the next section, we will start talking about ways to move up to the next section of the financial pyramid to the retirement funds section. Throughout this last chapter, I talked about Roth IRAs and 401(k)'s; if you do not know exactly what they are, then do not worry. This next chapter is almost completely devoted to these two tax classifications.

Retirement Planning

Planning for your retirement is essential in today's world. In the 1930s, the federal government decided that we needed to add social programs to benefit society. One of the most famous programs is Social Security. Social Security was developed to be the third leg of the retirement stool. Picture a stool in your mind; how many legs does it have to have to be stable? Of course, the answer is three, unless you have a huge one, but then I think it would be more of a stump. Anyway, this was the thought process behind Social Security. People should have some money saved for retirement—that is leg number 1. Companies used to have something called defined benefit programs or pensions—that was leg number 2. If the person worked long enough at the company, the company would pay a certain portion of their salary for a specified amount of time. The 1930s brought about an interesting economic situation. We have all probably heard of the Great Depression. Well, as the economy fell apart, companies began to go out of business. These were companies that paid pensions, so in reality, someone cut one leg off the retirees' stool. If the retirees had money invested in these companies through stocks, their savings suddenly disappeared, and there goes leg number 2. Many retirees were forced to go back to work, but with the massive layoffs, they could not find jobs. The government decided that we needed to change this. A country needed to take care of their elderly, so they gave the retirement stool another leg: Social Security.

Today we are seeing a transformation of the retirement stool once again. As the baby boom population begins to retire, we are finding that more and more companies simply cannot meet the defined benefits they promised. In fact, you are hard-pressed to find any company that offers a pension today. There is a very good reason for it too—they do not make economical sense. Today people are living longer than they ever have, well, except for those guys in the Bible that lived for nine hundred plus years, leaving companies with the responsibility of paying more and more money out to workers that are no longer contributing to any of the companies' profits.

401(k)

Companies still felt the need to offer some sort of retirement plan, probably not because they are really generous but rather to attract the best workers. The only solution that made sense was defined contribution plans. The most notable being the 401(k) for private companies and the 403b for nonprofit organizations. They are almost identical for the worker, so I will just say 401(k) for my examples. These plans force the worker to take an active part in planning for his or her retirement. The company says for every $1 you put in savings, we will match that $1 up to a certain percentage of your wage. So assuming you make $1,000 a month, I know that that is really low, but it makes the math easy. Three percent of $1,000 is $30. So if you put $30 a month into your 401(k) savings plan, the company will put an additional $30 into the account. This is the only way that I know of that you can give yourself a raise.

There as some limits on how much you can put into a 401(k) depending on your wage, but it usually caps at about 30% of your salary. Unfortunately, the company will only match up to the 3% of your wages; however, there are some tax advantages for using a 401(k). The government does not want to support you when you are old, so they give you an incentive to save now. Every dollar that you put into your 401(k) can be reduced from your income when you pay your yearly income taxes. If you use the example from above, you put $30 (3% of a $1,000) in a 401(k) you are only taxed on $970. This can be a major help to high-income individuals.

Sadly, Uncle Sam will not let you get away for free. The money in a 401(k) account cannot be pulled out and used until you are fifty-nine and a half years of age. The government says that this money is strictly for retirement. If you do pull it out before, you are hit with a minimum of a 10% fee, plus you must add the amount that you take out to your income for that year. After all the taxes and fees, you could lose as much as 50% of the value of what you withdraw. The other stipulation is that when you turn fifty-nine and a half and begin taking money, there are no more fees, but the money that you withdraw is considered income to you in those years. The government is giving you the opportunity to pull money out of your income tax free, and let it grow tax free, until you are ready to retire.

TRADITIONAL IRAs

Another retirement account that gives you tax benefits much like the 401(k), is the Traditional IRA. IRA simply stands for individual retirement account. You can probably deduce from the name that an IRA is solely the individual's responsibility. Your employer has absolutely nothing to do with your IRA. It is similar to the 401(k) in the fact that the money that you contribute to the traditional IRA is deducted from your income for that year. So if you make $10,000 and you put $1,000 in a traditional IRA, then your taxable income is reduced to $9,000. The major difference between the traditional IRA and the 401(k) is that you have complete control over the account and your employer does not match any of your contributions to your traditional IRA. The Traditional IRA, just like the 401(k), has the fifty-nine-and-a-half age requirement for withdrawals; so again, the government is giving you the opportunity to save money and let it grow tax free until you are ready to retire. An advantage that the IRAs have is that you have more choices for investment options. A 401(k) is usually limited to one fund family, and IRAs have virtually no limitations on any fund families. The main point is that IRAs give you more investment options.

ROTH IRA

Here is my favorite of the more common retirement accounts. The Roth IRA is designed on the same lines as the traditional IRA, but the tax laws are reversed. For the Roth IRA, you do not get any type of tax deduction for putting money into the account. If you make $10,000 and you put $1,000 in a Roth IRA, your taxable income is still $10,000. So you might be wondering why this is my favorite if there is no tax benefit for it. Well, there is a huge tax benefit when you turn fifty-nine and a half years old. Up to this time, you have been paying taxes on your money and then putting it into this account, and just like the other retirement accounts, you are not taxed on the interest it collects. At the magic age of fifty-nine and a half, you can begin pulling money out of your Roth IRA tax free! So every dime of interest you made over the last twenty to thirty years is not taxed at all. There are also some interesting rules around the Roth IRA that will allow you to pull your principal (money that you put into the account not interest earned) out earlier than fifty-nine years old. In addition, you have the increased investment options that I talked about with the traditional IRA—those rules apply for the Roth IRA as well.

You can also rest assured that the Roth IRA is a great financial planning tool because the government is trying hard to limit it. Right now for a young person, you are limited to $5,000-a-year contributions and $10,000 for a couple. The limitations are a little higher for people closer to retirement. I hope that the government will understand the power of this financial tool and lift the $5,000-a-year contribution level to much higher. This is probably not a reality since, if used correctly, people will literally have millions of dollars that is completely un-taxable. There is also another stipulation on the ROTH depending on your income. If you make more than $176,000 as a couple, you cannot contribute to the Roth IRA.

STRATEGIES

Now that we got all the boring definitions out of the way, we begin talking about how these accounts apply to everyday life. Think back to the three-legged stool. One leg was the defined benefit plans that we said is no longer available to workers. So now we have a two-legged stool: your savings and Social Security. I could take the rest of this book to discuss the arguments about if Social Security will be around or not when you are ready to retire. Personally, I believe that it is too important to society and it will be around, but again I do not want to go into an argument of why. I worked with several people that did not believe it would be around, so their retirement benefits were based solely on what they could save. If Social Security is around or not, it is almost assuredly not enough to live on. For us today, our lifestyle in retirement will depend upon how well we plan. Retirement planning is essential for financial well-being later in life, which is why it is the second level of our financial pyramid.

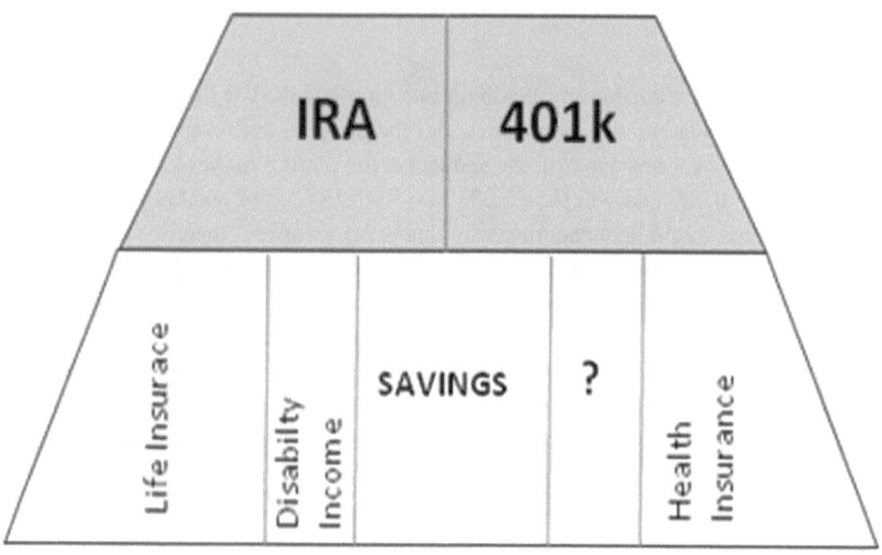

These two levels are by far the most important for your financial well-being. They are the two foundational levels that determine the rest of your life. If you look in the budgets I made in the previous chapter, you will see that I immediately began saving for retirement when I had three months of income in my emergency savings account. I wanted to finish the first tier and move to the second as soon as possible.

COMPOUNDING INTEREST

The sooner you can reach the second level, the better because of a little something called time value of money. This is the idea that the longer your money is in the market, or some other interest-bearing instrument, the wealthier you will become. Earlier I talked about avoiding credit card debt—because of interest, it will end up costing you more and more over time. Well, here we will begin using that same concept to our advantage. We know that the longer we have the debt, the more interest we have to pay. However, if we turn that around, we can see that the longer we have the money invested, the more interest we will make. Here is a basic example. You have $1,000 earning 10% interest for the year. At the end of the year, you now have $1,100. If you invest that whole amount at the same 10% interest rate for another year, you will have $1,210. The interest that you made in the first year has just paid you another $10. While $10 does not sound like a lot, you have to remember that it is money you generated without doing anything. If you keep reinvesting the original $1,000 and all the interest that it makes, in ten years that $1,000 becomes $2,593, over double of what you originally invested. Now comes the magical part: if you keep it in for an additional ten years, you will have $6,727. After thirty years, that $1,000 will grow to $17,450. The longer you have the money invested, the more wealth you will build. As you can see, the growth from twenty to thirty years is over $10,000 while the growth from ten to twenty years was only $4,700. This is because the more interest you can accumulate, the more interest it will pay. Compounding interest leads to what mathematics call exponential growth. The graph below gives an example of how this works.

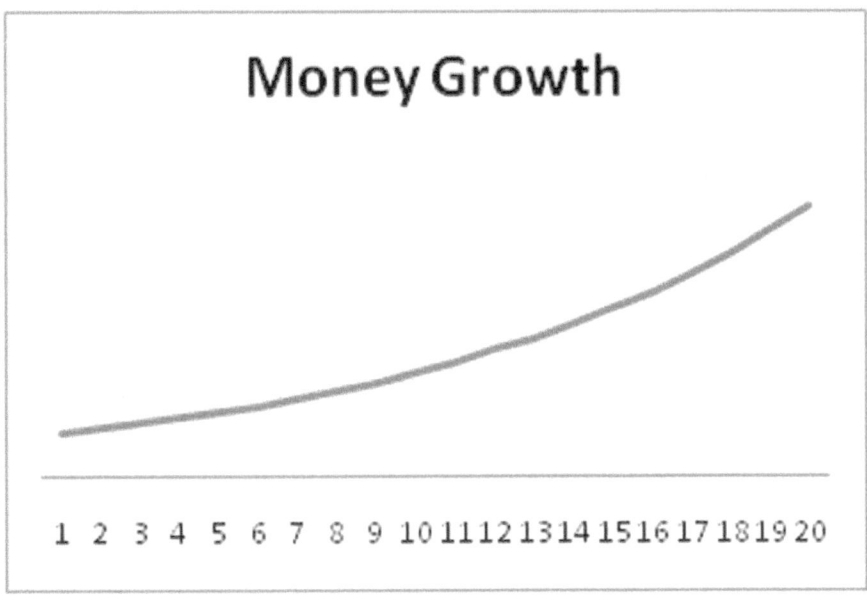

As you can see, the line become steeper as it gets closer to twenty years. The steeper the line, the faster your money is growing. From about year 14, your money is really beginning to grow rapidly. If we continued this line out for hundreds of years, we would find that the line would become so steep that it would seem to be going straight up. Unfortunately, most of us will need our savings at retirement and we cannot let it stay in the market for that amount of time.

Now that you can see the value in beginning to save for retirement as soon as possible, I hope you will understand why I said it will take a lot of discipline to finish the financial stability level as quickly as possible. You have to build that level before you can begin planning for retirement; otherwise, debt will eat away the money you have available to plan for retirement later in life. As we talked about in the budget chapter, you should be able to reach this point in fifteen months if you are willing to discipline yourself.

Once you reach this point, you now have three very good retirement vehicles available to you. So do you use all three? Just one? Which is the best? I will show you the ideal mix for the average young family. Starting with the 401(k) since it is the simplest to set up. You probably get a form from work that asks you how much you want to put away into a 401(k). Before you start looking at fund classes and stocks and bonds, you need to find out what percentage your employer matches you. Today 3% is the average. Whatever that percentage is, that is the amount you want to pull out to put in your 401(k). As I said earlier, you need to be saving at least 10% of your income. To maintain your emergency fund, you need to put 5% a month into that. If 5% is going into your savings account and 3% is going into your 401(k), which leaves at least 2% to go into your Roth IRA. If you have a 401(k), there is really no reason for the average individual to open a traditional IRA instead of a Roth IRA. Any extra money that you want to put away toward retirement should go in the Roth IRA, up to the $5,000-a-year-per-person limit.

You will find some people that disagree that you should max out your Roth IRA first. Their main point is that since you are working, your income is high, so you should maximize your tax deductions now, and this will give you more money to invest. While I think this is a good strategy, and if you take it, you will find that it will work well for you, I do not think it is the best plan. First of all, most people I know do not plan to be less wealthy as they get older. They plan to be wealthier. This means their income is going to be higher as they age. Here in America, we have something called income tax brackets. In 2009, the tax rates vary between 10% and 35% depending on your income. The less money you make, the lower your tax bracket, and the more money you make, the higher your tax bracket. So if you are planning on having more income as you age, when would it be best to pay the taxes on the income you will use for retirement? The answer is right now. If you can pay the taxes while you are still in a low tax bracket, then it will save you money in the long run.

The second reason is a bit more ambiguous. The United States has a relatively low income tax compared to most Western countries. Almost all the countries in Europe tax their citizens much heavier than the United States does. The reason for this is they offer many more state-supported services. In recent years, the United States has seen an increase in medical costs, Social Security, and many more social programs. If the United States government wants to continue offering these services, it must find a way to fund the increased costs. Another huge issue is the national deficit; currently it is larger than most of us can fathom and growing every day. The only solution that I can see is increased taxes over time. So right now your middle-class family is in about the 25% tax bracket; to keep up with escalating cost, the government may need to raise this closer to 40% similar to many of the European countries. If that is the case, it is much better to pay the tax today than in the future. While I do not have a crystal ball that can predict the future, this is the only scenario that I find to be logical.

If your spouse's and your taxable income is over $176,000 a year, then you cannot take advantage of the Roth IRA. Here you have a couple of options; one is to max out your 401(k) contributions. This works because the IRS only looks at your taxable income. Between you and your spouse, this should drop your taxable income at least $33,000 (the contribution rule changes every year). This is way over the 10% savings, but if you want to retire earlier, it is a good idea. The other is permanent life insurance. As I said, permanent life insurance is not good for most people. This is the exception. There are no income limits on life insurance, so you can save in it just like a Roth IRA.

SAVINGS GOALS

As we talked about earlier, you must attach your actions to some type of goal. Saving for retirement is not an exception to that rule. If you are putting money away for retirement, you need to have a goal for how much you want in retirement. There are two philosophies for how much you should save. The first is capital depletion. This is the idea that you save a bunch of money and then you spend it all in retirement. The second idea is capital retention. Here you save up *a lot* of money and then you live off the interest while in retirement.

Capital retention is by far the safest, so let's start with that. You need to figure out how much income you will need in retirement. Hopefully by this time, you will be completely debt free. So your income will strictly be to maintain whatever lifestyle you want. Once you have that decided, then think about charitable contributions, legacies for grandkids, etc. Try to envision what would make you the happiest in your retirement. Once you have everything, set down and total up what it would cost if you were to do it today. For example, I will use $100,000 a year as the total income number. Now we have a goal to reach for. If we use the capital retention philosophy, then we will need to grow our savings out and live off 5% of that a year. The 5% is the interest. This is a very conservative number; there is no reason that you cannot make 5% a year on average throughout retirement. The S&P 500 has averaged right over 8% for thirty years. So if you plan on living off of just 5%, you will not run into the risk of outliving your money. Back to the example, if we know that we need $100,000 a year in today's dollars, then we need to figure out what that will be thirty-five years from now when we retire. If we assume a 3% rate of inflation (the average rate), then we can see that in thirty-five years it will take $281,000 to have the same purchasing power that $100,000 has today. Again if you do not believe me, ask your parents how much basic living necessities were in the 1960s and 1970s and see how much 3% of inflation a year can raise prices. Now we have to plan on saving enough so that 5% of it is $281,000 or $5.6 million. To reach this goal, you would have to save $2,700 a month at 8% interest from age thirty to age sixty-five. To do this, you would have to max out your Roth IRAs for you and your spouse plus put $22,400 in your 401(k). For most people, this is not realistic, and for most people, they will not need $100,000 of income in retirement. Now I said that capital retention is the safest; with this you would never have to worry about running out of money if you lived to be 250 years old. Plus when you die, your kids will have $5.6 million to divide. However, if we look at the capital depletion model, we can find a more practical solution.

The capital depletion model starts out with a prediction of how long you think you will live. I would plan for one hundred. Most people do not live to see this age, so it should give you a good cushion. If we assume the same $100,000 in today's dollars, we can see how much we would need to save to reach our goal. That would still mean we need $281,000 a year starting in thirty-five years. So you will need to have $3.2 million in savings at age sixty-five and you cannot live past age one hundred. This means you will have to save $1,500 a month for retirement. A number that is much more manageable than the $2,700 that the capital retention plan requires.

Now as I said before, $281,000 a year is a lot for retirement income. Most people will not need that, and especially in the more advanced years of retirement. It can never hurt to save too much, however. The earlier you begin saving, the better. If you remember back to the budget example, I said that the couple needed to increase their Roth IRA contributions so that they were saving a total of $450 a month for retirement. This would give them $20,000 by the five-year goal. If that five-year goal would put them at age thirty, the $20,000 they have already saved would grow to about $300,000 by retirement age. This means they could cut their monthly retirement savings down by $150 a month for the next thirty-five years. Unfortunately, most of us do not have enough income to begin saving when we need to. The earlier you begin saving for the retirement, the less you will have to contribute.

FINDING YOUR TARGET

I want to step back to where I mentioned that you need to find a target income for your retirement. To do this, think of how much things cost in today's dollars. This means how much it would cost you to do it this year. So think about everything you want to do—some people want to retire and travel the world, some want to move to Florida, others want to pay their grandkids' way through college. Just try to think of everything you want to do and the legacy you want to leave behind. Remember, you are starting early so you can obtain some big, lofty goals. Next, look at your income now and see if you could accomplish all these goals with the income you have—the answer is more than likely no. This will give you an idea of what kind of income you will need to live on. Next, you need to think about major purchases and paying off debt. Do you want to make a major purchase such as a vacation home, etc., and most importantly, do you want to pay off your house early? The answer to this last part is yes and much sooner than the end of my thirty-year mortgage, but we will talk about that a little later. So if your mortgage is paid off, then that is more money that you can add to your disposable income. If you look back to the budget, you can see how much of an increase there would be in the entertainment section if you take out your mortgage and other debt. So remember, you will not have these expenses in retirement.

Once you have a good idea of how much income you will need in retirement, plus any major purchases, you can find a target savings number. Do all of these calculations just like you were going to pay for them today. Now you need to open up Microsoft Excel; if you do not have it at home, you probably have it at work or at the library. You need to first find out what impact inflation will have on these numbers. To do this, you need to know the rate of inflation; historically it has been right at 3%. So every year, prices increase at 3% on average. Then you need to know the number of years; if you are thirty and want to retire at sixty-five, it will be thirty-five years before you need this money. Now go to Insert (or Formula for Excel 2007) and click on Insert Function. Where it says search for function type in FV, it should look like this:

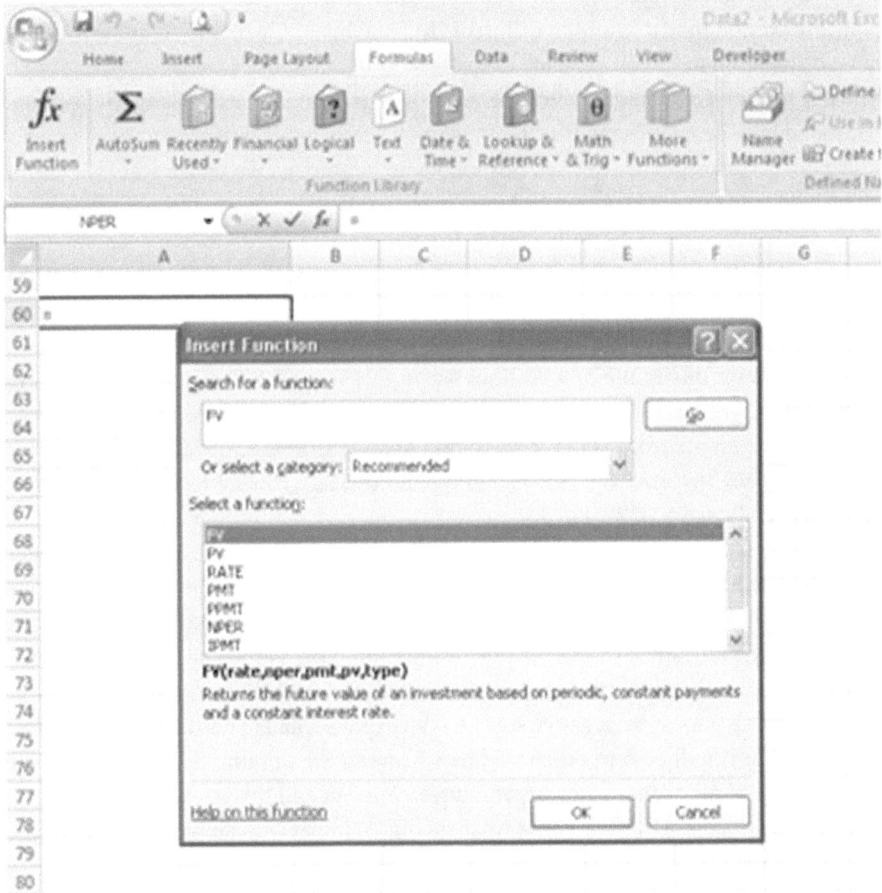

Then click OK. It will bring up five criteria: rate, nper, pmt, PV, type. Your rate is 3%, your nper or number of periods is 35, leave pmt or payments blank, your PV will be the number that you decided is your target income. Here you need to make that number negative since it is the amount that you will need to withdraw. Finally, leave type blank since you do not need it for this type of calculation. Once you have all this in, click OK and it will return the number into the cell you have selected. To let you know if you are doing it right, if you use 3% inflation for thirty-five years and you say you will need $100,000 in income, you should return a number of $281,386.25. This is the number that your target income will be equivalent to by the time you are ready to retire. If you look at the example, what it takes $100,000 to buy now will cost you $281,386.25 in thirty-five years.

So now we know how much we need each year in retirement. Now if you want to use the capital retention philosophy, it is very easy to figure out how much you will need to save. Simply take your target income and divide it by .05 or 5%. This will tell you your target savings goal. Again with the example, $281,386.25 / .05 = $5,627,724.91. The capital depletion model is a little different. To find this out, we need to use the present value calculation in Excel. Go back to the Insert Function, and instead of typing in FV type in PV, click Go, and then click OK. This will give you the exact same fields as the FV; the only difference is the PV option is not FV. To do this, we need to find a rate of return on the investment. We want this money to be safe, so we will use an 8% return, enter this for the rate. Next, you have to figure out how long you will live. This is the tricky part since none of us really knows. I recommend you plan to live to one hundred years, so subtract the age you plan on retiring from one hundred—this is the nper. If you want to retire at sixty-five, then you will need this income for thirty-five years. Finally, you will use the pmt, or payment section. You want a payment every year of your target income, so enter this in the pmt section. Again this will be subtracted from the value every year, so you need to make it a negative. Leave the FV and type sections blank. If you use the example from above, you should get a return of $3,279,435.19. So if you leave the money invested at 8% a year and pull out $281,386.25 a year for thirty-five years, you will need $3,279,435.19 to cover it.

Finding the cost of vacation homes and other major expenditures is done much the same way. If you want to buy a house in Florida or a Harley Davidson or a motor home, just look up what the price is today and then use the FV function in Excel again. Use 3% for the rate since that is the rate of inflation, nper is the number of years until retirement, leave the pmt area blank, and enter the cost of the expenditure today in the PV. Again this PV must be negative since it is an expense, and leave the type blank. This tells you what it will cost to purchase this when you are at retirement age. Once you have the cost of all of the major expenditures, you can add this to your target savings for retirement. This will give you a total savings number, the amount of money you need to have in the bank by the time you are ready to retire.

Now we need to determine how much to save each month so that you can reach your goal. To do this, you will use the payment function in Excel. Open up the Insert Function prompt—this time instead of using the FV or PV functions, you will type in PMT into the search. Click Go and then click OK. The first item is the rate, so now you need to decide what rate of return you are shooting for. If you are willing to take more risk, then you can shoot for a 12% return; if you want to be more conservative use the 8%. Next is Nper; this is the number of years you have until retirement. Leave PV blank unless you have money saved for retirement already. FV is your total savings number, and leave type blank. This will return how much money a year you need to save to reach your goal. Simply divide this number by twelve to get your monthly savings. Remember, this is the minimum savings each month. If you can put more away, it increases your chances for a better retirement.

This work here requires a good understanding of Excel. I hope you do not get lost in the formulas. If you do, this is a service that any financial advisor will perform free of charge. If you are planning on working with one, then I would not worry about trying the above calculations.

DISCIPLINE

Here we come right back to discipline. It is hard to bypass the nice cars, nice houses, boats, and other "toys"; but if you can learn to bypass them now, you can have them later in life, plus a much better retirement. I promise you, if your peers are out buying these things, they truly cannot afford them, and their lack of discipline will become evident when they begin thinking about retirement. Unfortunately, most people do not begin planning for retirement until age forty-five. If they do not start saving for retirement until then, they will have to contribute $2,000 a month more to have the same income as you in retirement.

There are a few people in my life that I really respect when it comes to financial matters. What these people told me helped shape my thinking about personal finance. The one story that stuck out the most was right after they graduated college and got married. They wanted to eliminate all of their credit card debts and begin saving. So for the first two years, they budgeted themselves $30 a month for entertainment. They admit it was tough when they had to forgo things that their friends were doing; however, today their biggest financial problem is deciding if they should buy a vacation home and wait until sixty to retire or pay off their home now and retire at fifty-five. Discipline is the key to obtaining your financial dreams. Now I will talk about the engine for your investment vehicles and how you can maximize it.

Investing

This is by far my favorite subject; as a financial advisor and a financial student, this is the section that intrigued me the most. I still remember my first investment class in college, the professor whom I would have to rank as one of the best I have ever had started the class out by asking, "How many people are here so that you could learn to be rich?" Of course, everyone in the class raised their hand; he then proceeded to tell us that he would teach us how we could make millions of dollars in the stock market. By now he had my full attention; I was expecting him to teach us to read charts and decipher head and shoulders and breakouts. I could see that all of my work learning the modeling and valuation formulas was finally paying off as I made millions of dollars in single transactions. He finished his thought by saying "over several years." For a nineteen-year-old college kid whose only future plans were to pass the class, find out what was going on that weekend, and get that blonde's number that was sitting across the room, several years meant by the time I was twenty-five. Unfortunately, his definition of several years and mine were nowhere close. The first example he gave had a time period of forty years! Right then he deflated my dreams of retiring at twenty-five to a warm, sunny beach.

As you read this section, I may have the disservice of deflating your dream as well. We all have heard the stories of people making millions on a single day of trading stocks; unfortunately, these occurrences are few and far between. The secret to becoming fabulously wealthy is compounding interest, not reading a chart. You will find day traders and even professional advisors that swear by charts. I have yet to see any conclusive evidence that trying to follow trends and buying stocks based on how the stock is following a certain pattern can generate higher returns than a buy-and-hold strategy. In fact, overall, this type of strategy usually leads to lower returns when you factor in your transaction costs. In addition, I would not recommend purchasing individual stocks right now. As you will see, individual stock is for farther up the financial pyramid. To begin your retirement investing, mutual funds are the primary vehicle.

MUTUAL FUNDS

The predominant investment philosophy today is the modern portfolio theory. This is a very statistical evaluation of stocks and bonds to figure out the best mix of both to give you the best return for the least amount of risk. Risk is the chance that you will lose money in the market, and return is how much you make in the market. We can all understand that the only reason we will take on more risk is if there is a good chance we can get a better return. Think of a poker game with three other people; if you raise the bet to $500, you just exposed yourself to a large risk of losing that $500. Conversely, you opened yourself up to the possibility of winning at least $500 from every person playing, as much as $1,500. You were willing to take the risk so that you could receive a higher reward. Well, modern portfolio theory says that you can still win $1,500, but you will only have to risk $200 to do so.

There is a lot of math behind this theory, but I will try to simplify it enough that you do not fall asleep and have to read this section three or four times. The simplest way to look at it is if you compare stocks and bonds. In theory, these two financial instruments are supposed to move opposite of each other. I talked about this briefly in the debt section; here I will explain it some more. If a company is doing well, then everyone wants to own stock in that company. As a stockholder, you have a small piece of ownership in the company. So if the company is growing and has great profits, you are entitled to a piece of that profit. The better the company does, the better the stock price does. In today's world, dividends are not really a factor. People, young people especially, buy stock for price appreciation, not dividends. Therefore, you want the company to do well so the price goes up. Conversely, if the company does poorly, then you want to own bonds, or the debt portion. Now there are several different types of bonds just as there are several different types of stocks, but for now just think of a secure bond. This means that you hold an IOU on the company, and if they cannot pay you, you have the right to force them to sell their assets to pay you. You are almost guaranteed to get paid even if the company does badly. Now look at how this would work over time.

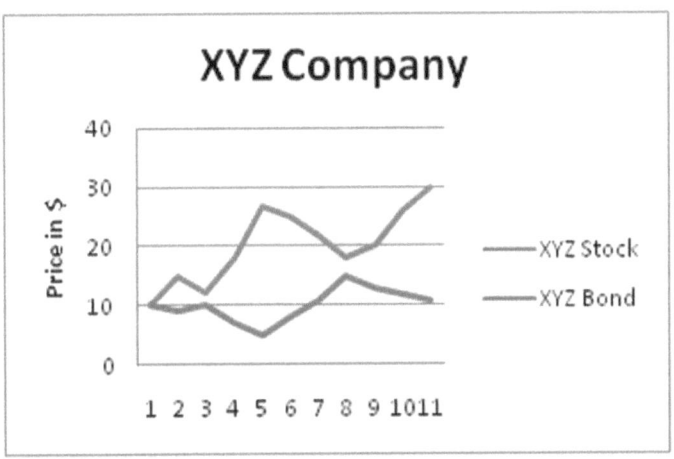

As you can see, when the stock price goes up, the bond price goes down, and when the stock price goes down, the bond price goes up. So if we graphed in the companies' profits, we would see that it is going up when the stock price is going up, and down when the stock price is going down. Now we can look at some investment strategies. If you had $2,000 to invest, you have several options—one is to buy all stocks. Assuming you bought two hundred shares at $10 and held them eleven years, your shares are now worth $6000. This is equivalent to a 15% return a year on your investment; however, this stock is very volatile. This means the price is up and down each year. The measure of risk is the standard deviation of the return; this means how close the return is to the average return, 15% in this case. The standard deviation for this stock over that time period is 29%. So for any given year, it would be common to see returns anywhere from negative 14% to as much as 44%. Some people do not mind this much risk, but most people do not want that big of a band. When you begin to add in some bonds, we can mitigate some of this risk. If you use that same $2,000 to buy seventeen shares of stock and three bonds, your return would be 13% and the standard deviation is 24%. So you would have to give up only 2% of return to drop your risk by 5%. As you add more bonds to your portfolio, your return will decrease slightly, but your risk will decrease drastically.

This is a very basic illustration of modern portfolio theory. Another factor that it addresses is systematic and unsystematic risk. Systematic risk is the risk that the whole market shares. Things such as recessions and depressions affect the whole market. So these are classified as systematic risk, and there is very little you can do to avoid it. Unsystematic risk, on the other hand, can be avoided. This is the risk that investors take on by not investing wisely. Here is a very common example. Many companies have stock purchase options for senior-level employees. These allow these managers to buy stocks at very good prices. Over time, a large portion of that person's portfolio is made up of one stock. Now if you think about how he or she is buying stock at a bargain, it might look like a shrewd investment move. Unfortunately, it exposes them to unsystematic risk. If the company they work for turns out to be Enron, for instance, the majority of their retirement savings could vanish almost overnight. The old adage "Don't put all your eggs in one basket" makes a lot of sense, especially when it comes to investments. You need to own stock in at least twelve companies so that your portfolio is diversified. Diversification completely nullifies unsystematic risk. Now you might be thinking that risk is not always a bad thing since it leads to higher returns. You are completely right when it comes to systematic risk. Unsystematic risk can give you extremely high returns; however, these returns almost always regress.

Increased systematic risk makes much more sense because of the competition in today's markets. Think of the technological sector. All through the 1990s, a company simply had to have some sort of technological reference in its name and its stock price would go through the roof. Then came 2001; the technological bubble popped, and many of these companies disappeared. If you had purchased stock in one of the hot new IPOs, you probably did very well through the 1990s only to watch your returns evaporate. However, if you had bought a wide range of stocks in the technological sector, there is a much better chance you would have bought an eBay, Google, Microsoft, Amazon, Apple, etc. These companies are still around today, and while your investment might have taken a hit, you would still have made money.

Mutual funds allow you to take advantage of all the benefits of modern portfolio theory without costing a fortune in transaction costs. There are two predominate ways to pay transaction costs: brokerage accounts and fee-based accounts. If you go to your financial advisor and tell him or her you want to open up an IRA, they will more than likely give you the option to open one of these accounts. A brokerage account means that you pay for each transaction that you make. So for every stock you buy, there is a small transaction cost. Think about what I said earlier; you need at least twelve stocks to diversify your portfolio. So every month when you make your contributions, you will pay twelve different transaction costs to buy each stock or bond that you want for your portfolio. These fees add up fast. So you have another choice: you can open a fee-based account and not pay any transaction costs but pay a 1-2% fee a year. Either way, you are going to pay a lot of fees. The best alternative is a brokerage account where you buy mutual funds. When you buy a mutual fund, what you are doing is giving a fund manager your money to go buy what stocks and bonds he feels is the best. What he can do is take your money, my money, and money from a million other people and go buy stocks. When he combines all of the deposits, he has enough money that he can buy these stocks in large quantities and thereby reducing the transaction costs for everyone. Now you can make one purchase and pay only one transaction cost for your mutual fund share and have a perfectly diversified portfolio with hundreds of stocks and bonds.

Your only problem is deciding on which mutual fund to buy. All mutual funds are not the same. Morningstar does a great job of ranking and monitoring mutual funds. It will give you the past performance of the fund manager, the investment strategies, fees, and much more. Your biggest concern is the return over time and fees. If the fund is returning 10% a year, that is great, but if it charges 4% in fees, then you can probably find something better. There are three basic share classes with different fee schedules.

A CLASS

A class shares require you to pay a certain fee up front to purchase them. They are called front load funds. Let's just use 1% for a number. So if you want to invest $10,000 in an A class mutual fund, it will cost you $100 up front. These are good funds for long-term investments. The yearly fees are usually lower, so you can make up for the extra cost up front. As I said earlier, your best strategy for retirement accounts is to buy and hold. So A class shares make sense.

B CLASS

B class shares require you to pay a fee when you pull the money out of the account. They are usually called rear load funds. One good thing about the B class share is that when you buy it, there are no up-front costs. So if you want to invest $10,000, you can invest $10,000. In addition, fund managers like you to keep your money with them. The more money they have under management, the more they get paid. Therefore, they will give you incentives to keep the money with them as long as possible. After several years, and I mean several, the B class share turns into an A class share. What that means for you is that if you keep your money in for a long time, you will not have to pay fees up front or when you pull the money out. This seems like a great deal, and in many cases, it is. Just make sure you pay attention to fees since you have to pay them every year no matter what.

B class shares are becoming more and more uncommon, however. The reason is that they expose the financial advisor to more risk since it costs people extra money to pull their money out of these funds. Take, for instance, a scenario where you bought a B class share and it performs very badly, causing you to lose a significant amount. Now you have a dilemma; do you pull the money out right now and take the loss plus pay an additional termination fee, or do you let it ride? Many times people feel that the termination fees force them to make bad investment decisions, so they sue their financial advisor for putting them in a B class share in the first place.

C CLASS

The final share class is the C class. This is commonly referred to as the no-load funds. There is no cost to purchase the fund or to sell the fund. Before you begin thinking that this is the fund for you, you have to know that the yearly fees for C class shares are the highest. There is no free lunch. These are the best funds for short-term investments since they are no-load funds and the yearly fees will not have much time to eat away at your returns. However, retirement saving is for long term. So over twenty to thirty years these increased yearly fees will eat away at your returns. I would not recommend C class shares unless the fund performance is extremely good.

With any share class, you need to pay attention to the yearly fees. One major fee is the 12b-1 fee. This is the marketing fee, so in actuality, this fee does nothing for you. It is simply the fee you pay so that the company will have money to market this fund. Look very closely at the prospectus—it will tell you all of the fees you are paying and what they are for. Some companies, such as Vanguard, have made a reputation for themselves of keeping these fees very low. However, fees are not the most important thing. A fund that has a very good performance history will be worth a little higher fee.

MARKET CAPITALIZATION

Now that you understand the value of mutual funds and the different share classes, we can start looking at different types of mutual funds. Before we look at fund families, we need to start looking at what sectors of the market you should invest in.

To start out, we can look at the equity or common stock portion. These are the stocks that you think of when someone says the "stock market." On the stock market, the shares are divided into three large categories. One is large market capitalization stocks (large cap), then there is medium market capitalization stocks (mid cap), and finally small market capitalization stocks (small cap). The difference in the three is their market capitalization. This is simply the number of shares outstanding multiplied by the stock price.

Large cap stocks are usually the big corporations with a long history behind them. To be considered a large cap, the company needs a market capitalization of over $10 billion. Next, I want to skip to small caps; these are the smaller companies with a market capitalization of less than $2 billion. Small cap stocks are usually newer companies that are still relatively small.

Then there is mid cap stocks; these are the companies with a market capitalization between $2 billion and $10 billion. In theory, these are the companies that are medium sized. However, in many cases, they are either small cap companies on their way to being large cap companies or large cap companies that are falling to small cap companies.

There are mutual funds in each one of these categories. You can find funds that are made up of just large cap stocks, just small cap stocks, or just mid cap. Mid caps are less common since they are many times stocks in transition from large to small cap stocks. There are also balance funds that utilize all three categories. What you need to know about each one is the risks and rewards associated with each. Take large cap stocks, for instance; these are the very large solid companies. For the most part, they have been around for a hundred years and should be around for the foreseeable future. If you think back to when we talked about risks and returns, you will remember that risk is the chance you will lose your money. Large cap stocks are considered the safest stocks that you can invest in. Therefore, the risk associated with large cap stocks is the lowest of all three categories. This also means that, overall, the return is the lowest on these stocks. Now you need to remember that all stocks are risky investments. Stock prices vary every day, and there is no guarantee that any company will be in business next week, which is why the returns in the stock market are higher than anywhere else. However, if any company should stay in business, it is a large cap.

Small cap stocks are the exact opposite. If a business is going to fail, it is usually in the first few years. So small cap stocks are the most risky of the three categories, but they offer the largest potential returns. Most of the companies you think of are large cap stocks, even when they first went public. Think of Google when it had its initial public offering—it had an initial market capitalization of $23 billion right from the start. A small cap stock is for a company that is truly a small business, and as a small business, they are much more volatile. To understand why, compare the effect of $1 billion of net income, or profit, to a large company and a small company. If we take GE, who has been around for over one hundred years, they had a net income of $17.410 billion in 2008. So another $1,000,000,000 of net income would raise it to $18.410 billion or an increase of 5.73%. Now look at a small cap stock like XYZ Company (there is an actual company, but I do not want to get sued for using their name)—its net income was $135 million in 2008. If we added that same $1 billion of net income, it would increase its net income by 740%. Net income is usually the starting point for most valuation formulas, so as you can see, increases in profit for small cap companies has a much bigger effect than for large cap companies. If the net income of this company increased by 740%, XYZ Company's stock price would go from $12.85 to $107.78 overnight. The converse is also true: if each company happened to lose $1 billion, it would only affect GE's net income by 5.73%, but it would completely bankrupt XYZ Company.

Another way to measure the riskiness of the stock is to look at the beta. The beta is a key concept in the capital asset pricing model (CAPM) formula; I could take the rest of the book to explain CAPM, but all you really need to know is beta. Beta is how well the stock follows the "market." Most generally, the market is the S&P 500 index, so if your stock has a beta of 1, it will go up 1 point when the market as a whole goes up 1 point. Conversely, it will go down 1 point when the market as a whole goes down 1 point. Large cap stocks have a beta close to 1; small cap stocks have a beta greater than 1. So back to company XYZ Company, it has a beta of 1.65. This means that if the market goes up 1 point, XYZ Company's stock goes up 1.65 points. This is great as long as the market is going up. For every $100 the market is making, you are making $165. Unfortunately, when the market loses $100, you lose $165. It is considered more risky.

The main concept that I want you to come away with from this whole section is that large cap stocks are generally the safest stocks to invest in, while small cap stocks are the most risky stocks to invest in.

YOUR PORTFOLIO

Now that we got all the educational (boring) parts out of the way, we can start talking about what your portfolio should look like. Since this book is geared for young people, the investment portfolio I will show you targets growth. It is a portfolio that exposes you to a lot of risk, but it gives you the potential for high returns. Since you have a longtime horizon, you can afford to expose yourself to risk.

Over the stock market's history, it has averaged 8%. Average is the key. There probably has not been more than two years in all of history that the stock market has actually returned 8% in a year. There are years when the stock market saw huge growth of over 20%, and there are years when it lost over 20%. Yet overall, if you average everything out, it comes out to 8% a year. As a young person, you have the time to ride out the big swings and get the average return over time. The 8% is the market as a whole; this portfolio will favor small cap stocks that we hope will outperform the market.

Aggresive Retirement Portfolio

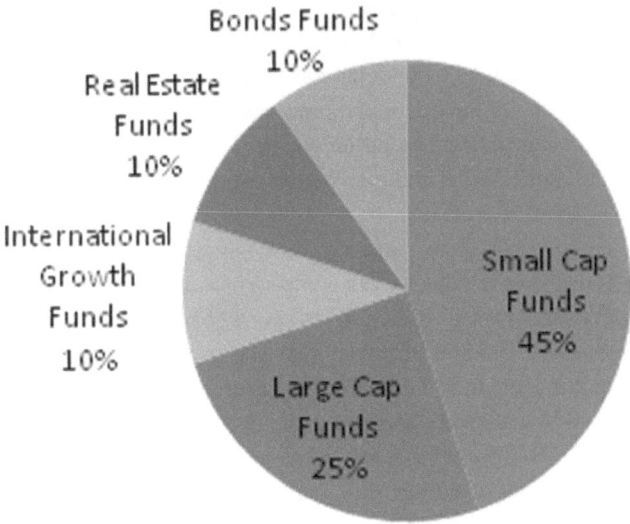

This portfolio allocates 80% of your investments into more aggressive funds. So for every $1,000 you invest, $800 of it goes into "risky" funds and $200 goes into more conservative funds. The International Growth Fund is investing in stocks of companies that are located outside the United States. These funds are usually centered more around emerging markets such as South East Asia and Latin America. However, there are funds that look for value in more established markets such as those in Europe. Overall, international funds are considered more risky than large cap funds, just like small cap funds. This portfolio is shooting for a much better return than 8%; in fact, small cap funds averaged right around 12% up until 2006. The market has been all over the place since then, but we can assume that this will be corrected with time.

Now I have to give you the justification for taking this risk. To do this, I need you to think back to the "Retirement Planning" section. In there, I talked about finding a target income for retirement and then planning on saving toward that goal. For the example, I used $100,000 in today's dollars as the target income. To accomplish this, I showed that you would have to save $1,500 a month for thirty-five years. That was assuming the average market rate of 8%. Since you are young, we can use the above portfolio and push for a higher return. If we used the exact same numbers from the previous example but invested it at 12%, you now only need to invest $240 a month to reach your target of $2.3 million in your retirement account. In addition, if you remember back to that $20,000 I suggested you save by the five-year goal, that $20,000 invested at 12% turns into $1 million.

This is where the discipline I have been preaching about really pays off. I showed you earlier that if two people both needed the same target income for retirement but one started in his or her twenties and the other person waited until his or her forties, the one that started in his forties would have to invest $2,000 a month more. At that time, I just wanted to illustrate how compounding interest made such a drastic difference. For that illustration, I showed each person investing at 8%. Now I can bring in another variable, the idea of taking on more risk for a higher return. If that person waits until his forties to begin investing, he will not have as much time to ride out the market. This means that since they do not have as much time, they cannot invest as aggressively as the person that starts at age thirty. The earlier you begin investing, the more risk you can take, which leads to much higher returns. We are using the "magic" of compounding interest at a much higher interest rate.

As you saw earlier, that 4% increase in return over thirty-five years makes a huge difference on your investment. Now we can compare how much it will save you to begin investing for your retirement at age thirty. If you save $240 a month for thirty-five years, you will have a total of $100,800 of money that you contributed to the account. The rest of the value in this account is the interest you accrued over those thirty-five years. Now if you wait until you are forty and you only have twenty-five years to invest, you will have to invest $3,740 a month to reach the same target income for retirement. This totals out to be $1,121,000 of money that you will have to put into the account. By beginning saving at thirty, you will save yourself $1,020,200! As you can clearly see, the earlier you begin saving for retirement, the less it will cost you. If you begin saving at age twenty-five, then you will have to save even less. Think about that extra $1 million that you will have from age forty to age sixty-five. Your discipline today will give you an extra $41,000 a year from age forty to age sixty-five.

REAL ESTATE

Now we need to look back at the portfolio. There is still 20% that we have not covered: the real estate and the bonds. Real estate is pretty simple since we are all familiar with it. What you might not be familiar with is how the average person can invest in real estate. There are two types of funds that are very common: one is a REIT or real estate investment trust, the other is a real estate fund. Both of them act a lot like a mutual fund. There is a person or a team of individuals who collects a little bit of money from a bunch of people until there is enough money for them to go out and buy properties. Some of them are focused on developing the land; others are more focused on generating income through rental properties. However, either way, real estate has been a great investment for the last thirty years even with the cyclical downturns in the market. You can find lists of REITs and real estate funds, and if you are working with a financial advisor, he will have a list of recommendations for you.

BOND FUND

The other 10% of the portfolio is the bond fund. There are many different types of bonds, but to simplify it, I will put them into three main categories: government bonds, corporate Bonds, and municipal Bonds. The government bonds that you are probably most familiar with are the zero-coupon bond. These bonds are the type that you pay $50, wait for about seven years, and then go give the bank the paper, and they give you $100. During those seven years, you pretty much forget about the bond.

Corporate bonds, on the other hand, have a coupon payment. This means that once or twice a year, the company has to pay you a certain amount of interest.

Municipal bonds can work either way. There are also different taxes for each one. The state and federal governments made a compromise that the issuer of the bond would also tax the bond. So if you cash in a government bond for $100 and you only paid $50, the federal government requires you to pay taxes on the $50 you made. The good part is that you do not have to pay any state taxes on the profit. Likewise with municipal bonds, since they are issued by the city, county, or state, you do not have to pay any federal taxes. The best part of municipal bonds is that many states give you an added incentive to invest in your local community by waiving the taxes on profits from municipal bonds. So in reality, your investment is completely tax free. Corporate bonds do not have any of these advantages since they are issued by a corporation. Therefore, the profits from corporate bonds are taxed by both the federal and state.

Since this portfolio is for retirement income, it is in a qualified account. A qualified account is a Roth IRA, traditional IRA, 401(k), etc., all the accounts that allow you to invest money and let it grow tax free. With the money already sheltered from taxes, there is no real tax benefit for any of the three choices. Your main concern when looking at bond portfolios is the return. I would suggest high-grade corporate bond funds. Corporate bonds are graded as to how financially secure the company is, so the better the rating, the more likely the company will not go out of business anytime soon. Just remember, the better the rating, the less risk; and the less risk, the lower the return.

RISK TOLERANCE

There is just one more area about risk that we need to cover, and that is risk tolerance. Risk tolerance is the amount of risk that you can comfortably take on. The portfolio that I suggested is about the riskiest portfolio that I would ever suggest to anyone. However, since this book is geared for young people, I think that the return will justify the risk. This portfolio will make major swings in values over a ten-year period. There will be years that the value will be down significantly and years that the returns will be phenomenal. The key is that you have time to ride out all the big swings and go for the long-term return. Nevertheless, I have talked to enough people to know that just because you are young does not mean that you will want to take on high risk. There are some personalities that cannot handle seeing these huge swings in their portfolio's value. If you feel that this is the case for you, then I would not recommend the portfolio from above. I think that this is the optimal portfolio for anyone from their twenties all the way up until age forty, but if you are losing sleep at night over the value of your retirement accounts, then you should probably go to a safer portfolio such as this one:

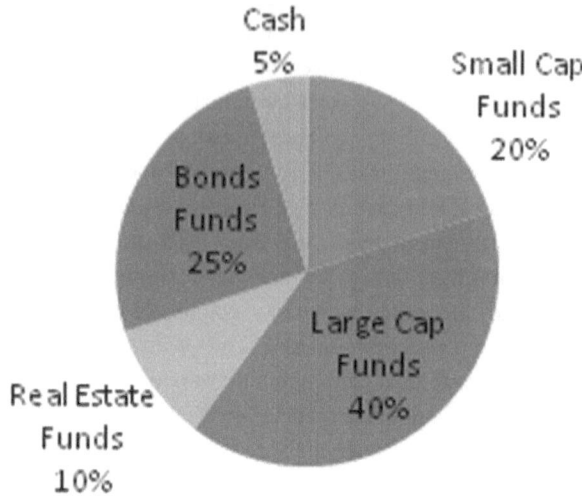

Conservative Retirement Portfolio

Cash 5%

Small Cap Funds 20%

Bonds Funds 25%

Large Cap Funds 40%

Real Estate Funds 10%

This portfolio increases your exposure to bonds and cash. By cash, I mean money market accounts, not actual cash under your bed or buried in a coffee can outside. There is no exposure to international stocks, and the small cap funds are reduced to 20%. The majority of your investment is in large cap funds. Remember these are the safest of the risky investments. This portfolio still has the potential for very good returns; however, you will not see the drastic value changes.

FUNDS

Now that you know how to divide up your portfolio, you can decide which funds to buy. There are two different philosophies for fund management. The first is actively managed funds. These are the funds that have a fund manager whose sole responsibility is trading stocks daily to make sure that the fund outperforms the market as a whole. The second philosophy is passively managed funds. These are the funds that the fund manager goes in and buys a wide selection of funds in a certain sector and then holds on to them. Unlike the actively managed funds, there is no trading.

Now the question is, which philosophy is better? Well unfortunately, the answer is both. There are actually some fund managers out there that are very good. They do their homework, find good sectors in the market to invest in, and most importantly, they can avoid potentially dangerous sectors. The only bad part is these good fund managers usually want to get paid for being good. In addition, there are much more transaction costs with actively managed funds.

Overall, the funds that are actively managed have higher yearly fees than the passively managed funds. This makes sense when you think about the work that is put into the actively managed funds. So the hard part is finding a fund that is outperforming the market by a percentage that is higher than its cost in fees. Say, for instance, that you find a fund that has averaged 9% for the last thirty years. Well, when you compare it to the market, the fund manager looks like a genius. He has beaten the market over thirty years. Then you dig through the prospectus and find that the sum of the yearly fees is 3%. This actually reduces your return to 6%, 2% below the market, and you have already seen how much of a difference 2-4% can make over thirty years.

When you look at the funds, pay specific attention to their average returns and their yearly fees. If you find a fund that has outperformed the market consistently by a percentage that is higher than its yearly fees, then it is a good buy. Conversely, if you cannot find a fund that has done so, then buy the passively managed funds. The best passively managed funds are index funds. These funds are mirror images of a certain index. Take a large cap fund, for instance; this would be a mirror image of the S&P 500 index. So whatever the S&P 500 does, this fund would match it perfectly. You can buy index funds for international funds, small cap funds, and large cap funds. The fees are inexpensive, which is one of the main reasons I like them. No matter which type of fund you choose, use a buy-and-hold strategy. This means that it does not really matter what the market does day to day—your goal is a long-term retirement goal, and your investment strategy matches it. So do not pay attention to the stock market's close every day; this will only drive you crazy. You want to buy the fund now and hold on to it for thirty years. It does not matter what the fund does day to day; the important part is what it is returning over ten, fifteen, or twenty years. Remember mutual funds are way too expensive to be trading unless the fund manager has gone completely crazy.

ETFs

Another alternative to an index fund is an ETF or exchange traded fund. ETFs came around because sometimes it is expensive to invest in a mutual fund. We talked earlier about A, B, and C shares plus the yearly fees that each one has. Well, ETFs eliminate this problem. What they do is take a mutual fund and divide it into one hundred parts. They then take these individual parts and sell them on an exchange just like a stock. Now you can buy the ETF without paying any load fees and the yearly fees are almost nonexistent. These are usually very inexpensive to begin investing in and very easy to buy. My advice to you starting out is to utilize ETFs. Since you do not have a lot of money to purchase mutual funds right now, take advantage of the cheaper products. Once you have $20,000 invested, then you can start looking at mutual funds. The reason for this is there are price breaks for the more money you invest in the mutual fund. Also if you do not want to take the time to research hundreds of mutual funds, your safest alternative is to buy index funds or ETFs from these indexes.

MONTHLY INVESTING

Another important part of investing is consistency. The best way to invest is by putting money away every month. I have actually met people that only put money into their IRAs at the end of the year when they are filling out their taxes. Now I think it is good that they are putting money away; however, it would be better if they had planned to do this every month. The reason for this is something called dollar cost averaging. We all know that the stock market is volatile on a day-to-day basis—one day it may be up, the next it may be down. So if you invest every month, sometimes the prices will be up and sometimes they will be down, but overall, you will get an average that is about medium.

Another advantage to monthly contributions is it helps mitigate losses. The best example I have ever heard for this was the Air Force Academy cadets from the class of 2001. As cadets, they receive a loan during their junior year that is almost interest free. So the class of 2001 received their loans during 2000, at which time the market was posting astronomical returns. It seemed like a sure bet that if they invested the amount in the stock market, they could double, if not triple, their money in just a few short years. Unfortunately, some cadets dumped the whole loan amount into the market only to watch the market free-fall. It would have taken them almost six years to recoup their losses. Had they put the money in little by little, they would have been buying as the prices were dropping. This would have lowered their cost, but it would have also given them the opportunity to avoid investing until the stock market corrected itself. Now the opposite is also true. They could have picked the best time possible and made millions. They could have also taken the money to Vegas and hit the royal flush three times in a row. Both of which are very unlikely.

Investing on a monthly basis also keeps your investment balanced. When I gave you the portfolios, they have specific percentages for each group. Unfortunately, the market changes every day, so the only time your portfolio will be perfectly balanced is the day that you buy the stocks. The small cap funds might lose some money, and the large cap gain; this will change up your portfolio's balance. In order to rebalance the portfolio, you must sell the funds that are performing very well and buy the ones that are not performing well. This may not make sense initially, but think about the key to investing: buy low, sell high. That is exactly what you are doing. Unfortunately, this will bring on more transaction costs and fees. If you are putting money in each month, you will automatically rebalance the portfolio. If the small caps' value is down, that means you will be able to buy more of them with the same amount that you invested last month. In addition, if the large cap funds' value is up, you cannot buy as much as last month. Over time, this will keep the portfolio from being skewed too far in one direction since you are buying a lot when it's low and a little when it's high.

401(k) INVESTING

Investing in a 401(k) is somewhat different from an IRA. With an IRA, you have the choice of almost any fund you want to invest in; but with a 401(k), you are limited to one fund family. You can still use the portfolio that I have given you above; you just have to stick to the funds that they offer. There should be more than one fund for each sector, so again, find the funds that give you the best return with the lowest cost. The 401(k)'s also usually offer investment classes such as growth, moderate growth, conservative, etc. These are just portfolios like the one above. Their definition of conservative and mine will differ greatly since this book is geared for younger people with more time to invest. I would still recommend my portfolio above; however, many people do not have the time to find the best funds. In that case, use the most stock intensive portfolio the fund family offers you.

The 401(k)'s also have an ownership aspect to them such as an IRA once you make it past the vesting period. The vesting period is different for every company; some companies say you are fully vested as soon as you start. *Vesting* is another word for ownership. The vesting period is the time it takes before you are the 100% owner of all the contributions that the company makes to your account. Other companies may say the vesting period is three years, but you gradually own more each year. So assuming you contribute $10,000 to your 401(k) a year and the company matches you 3%, at the end of a three-year period, you will have $900 in your account that the company contributed. If you are fully vested at that time and you quit your job, you are allowed to take that whole $900 with you. If at that time you were only 50% vested, then you could only take $450 of those contributions. So what this means for your retirement accounts is that once you are fully vested, you are the sole owner of the account. This is something that did not happen with pensions. In the past, the companies owned the pension account, and you were subject to their rules on how you could access the money. Today if for some reason you leave your job and you are fully vested, you can take your 401(k) accounts with you.

Unfortunately, if you are not fifty-nine and a half, you still cannot access this money without some penalties. So if you take the money out in cash and go buy a car or house, you are going to get a really big tax bill. To compensate for this, the IRS gives you an option to keep the money for retirement. If you go back to the section where I defined 401(k)'s and IRAs, you will see that I said the 401(k) is very similar to the traditional IRA. Therefore, you can take the money from your 401(k) and roll it over into a traditional IRA. This is usually a good thing because now that the money is classified as an IRA, and you are not tied to one fund company, now you can explore thousands of other investment opportunities. By the time you retire, you will probably have switched companies a few times; this means you will have a couple of traditional IRAs, a 401(k) from your last job, and a Roth IRA.

TIME VALUE OF MONEY

I want to reiterate that time is very important to you obtaining your financial goals. The earlier you can begin investing, the easier you can obtain your goals. The sacrifices you have to make now will be rewarded in time. If you can discipline yourself to save when you are at the beginning of your career, you can enjoy the money that you make when you are advanced in your career. Most people do not understand this concept. They tend to want to have fun and buy all the nice things when they are young. Then save for retirement as it gets closer. I hope you understand that if you do it that way, it ends up costing you much, much more. Let the interest you earn build up your retirement account, not just the money you put away. This will allow you to do other things with the money you are making in the prime of your career. It may be hard work now, but it will be worth it in the future.

Stocks and Bonds

Once you have your retirement funds in place, you need to begin saving in unqualified accounts. Unqualified accounts are accounts that you can access before fifty-nine and a half without surrender penalties. IRAs and 401(k)'s are classified as qualified plans. Saving in unqualified accounts is level 3 on your financial pyramid.

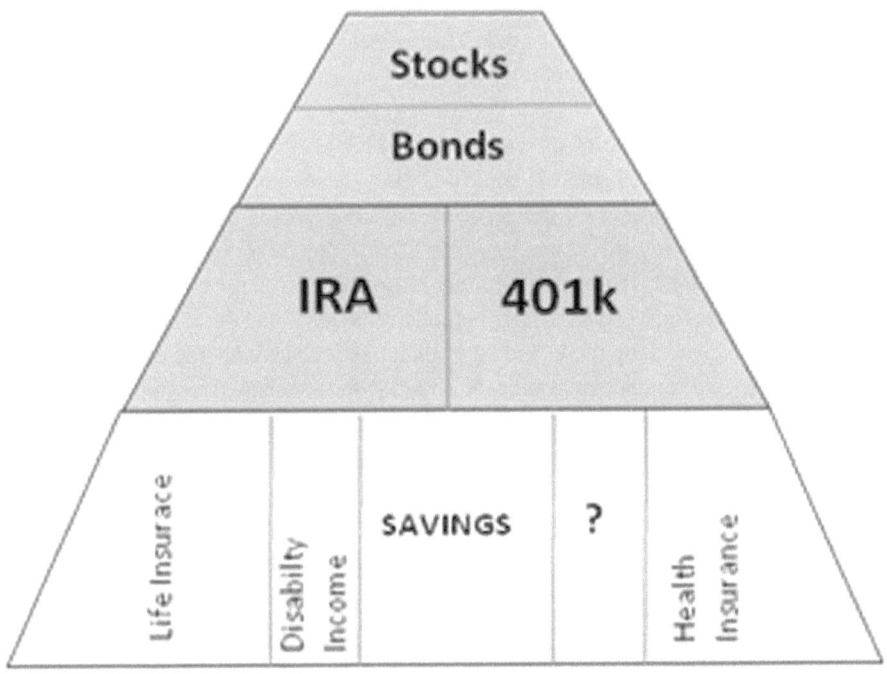

Ideally, you should be about seven years into this process when you reach level 3. You should already have a significant nest egg set aside for retirement, and your income should be growing. In an ideal situation, your income will grow enough that the 5% you are putting away for retirement will be more than you need to invest each month to reach your retirement goals. Once this becomes the case, you can begin looking at unqualified accounts. These accounts usually have shorter-term goals attached to them, things such as saving for your kids' college tuition, buying a car, a boat, etc. These are not short-term goals because you never want to enter the market if you are going to need the money in less than five years. Five years should give you enough time to get a good return and ride out any downtimes. The advantage of this level is that you can actually access the money without losing so much to penalties. The disadvantage is that this money is taxable. So if you own stocks that pay dividends, you have to pay taxes on the dividend. Also, if you sell any stocks that appreciated in the market, you will have to pay taxes on any gains. For this section, your investments should be weighted more toward stocks than bonds at your younger age. As you get older, this may change to a fifty-fifty split between stocks and bonds.

STOCKS

For this section, I would recommend the majority of your investment be in large cap stocks, with some small cap and international to give you a little boost. At least 75% of your investments should be in large cap. You want to take advantage of the stock market's returns, but you also want to reduce risk. This money does not have the thirty-year time horizon that your retirement accounts have, so you want to take a more conservative approach.

Buying stocks takes a lot of research and a lot of time to do correctly. The big investment managers have teams of people that study the market and financial statements. Most of us do not have time for this since we have our lives to live. So the best advice I can give you is to buy the things you like. If you like Target better than Wal-Mart, buy the stock in Target. If you think people at Nordstrom are nicer than the people at Macy's, buy Nordstrom. The reasoning behind this is that if you think it is a better store, you are more likely to shop there, and more than likely you are not the only person that feels that way. Buy things that you know about. I, for instance, like motorcycles, and especially Harley-Davidsons. So I know the models that are out now, and I have looked at the models that will be coming out next year. Riding is my hobby, and researching the company is just an extension of that hobby. It does not take me long to look at the new bikes coming out and what kind of market I think there will be for them; in addition, I love doing it. It gives me a reason to go down to the Harley shop and look at new bikes. Your investments should be the same way. Invest in things you like and you know about. You do not need to know the P/E value or the beta of the stock. Let the day traders and professional traders worry about that.

The other piece of advice I can give you is not to day trade. First of all, the fees that are associated with the trading are very high. If you open a generic account from ShareBuilder or E-Trade, they offer you a few different packages. If you plan on day trading, it will cost at least $30 a month for your account. In addition, there is something called a bid-ask spread. This is the difference in what you pay for the stock and what you can sell the stock for. This spread can change every few seconds, but it is generally anywhere from $0.10 to $0.20. The spread is where floor traders make money, and they end up making a few cents on every trade. Let us assume that you make one trade of fifty stocks a day. In a year, you will have paid a minimum of $360 in expenses. If you have $10,000 invested, you will have to make at least 3.6% to cover your costs. Now think back to what I talked about earlier with the market as a whole averaging 8%. To match the market, you will have to make 11.6%. In addition, the bid-ask spread would eat away about .1% of your returns. Buying and holding the stocks makes much more sense, and a lot of the accounts have provisions that if you set it up on a monthly withdrawal, they will not charge you transaction fees at all.

After thinking about all the work that goes into buying stocks, many people choose to fund this section with mutual funds. They already have experience choosing mutual funds, so they will just let the experts buy the stocks. If you choose to do this, you may find that there are a couple of funds in your retirement accounts that are performing very well, now is a good time to capitalize on them. However, you need to pay close attention to the way the fund distributes gains. Some funds will actually distribute dividends or income to the shareholders; if this is the case, you will be taxed on this income. Otherwise, you will only be taxed on any gains when you sell the funds.

BONDS

The other part of section 3 is the bond portfolio. There are two reasons for adding bonds. One, we have already talked about how bonds can limit risk while maintaining high returns. The other reason is that these funds are unqualified accounts, so we can take advantage of some of the tax laws. Municipal bonds are not taxed on the federal level by law, and the state taxes them on the state level. However, most states want its denizens to invest into their local community. To accomplish this, they will waive all taxes on income from municipal bonds issued within the state or by the state. In essence, you are creating tax-free income. Since the profits in this account are taxable, you will want to mix in municipal bonds to lower your tax liability. In addition, since municipal bonds are not taxed on the federal level, federal bonds are not taxed on the state level. So if you mix in federal bonds, it will lower your tax liability but not as much as municipal bonds since they are still taxed at the federal level. I would incorporate a mixture of 40% municipal, 20% federal, and 40% corporate investment grade bonds.

I would not recommend that you try to buy individual bonds by yourself. For this section, I would say use bond funds. They are just like mutual funds, but they are managed by professionals. The bond market can be tricky for the simple reason that the information is not as readily available as it is for the stock market. Think about the last time you heard an update on the bond market on the news. It probably has been a long time ago, if ever. The stock market is "sexy," so you get updates on the Dow and S&P all the time, but it is a little harder to find information on the bond market.

SECTION 3

Once you reach this section, I want you to know that you have set yourself up to be extremely wealthy. If you can discipline yourself enough to make it through the first two sections, you can now allow yourself to live a very good lifestyle. Before, I talked about an emergency savings account with three months of income; its sole purpose is to keep you out of debt when emergencies arise. These accounts now will keep you out of debt when opportunities arise.

Section 3 of your financial planning allows you to "bank on yourself." Imagine that you want to buy a nice BMW and you actually have enough money to pay cash for it. That is what this account is establishing; you are planning ahead for major purchases. So instead of buying it now and paying tons of interest for the next five years, you are saving now and letting the interest build up your principal. This account should continue to grow into your forties and fifties until you can almost make any purchase you want with cash.

COLLEGE SAVING

If you want to pay for your kids' college, then here is the perfect time to begin that. You should have at least ten years to save, so let the interest help build up your account, instead of paying interest on the loans that you take out. In addition, there are several good savings plans available that actually allow you to defer some of your income into these accounts and reduce your taxes. The major drawback to these is they have to be used for college or else you face major fees and penalties.

Collectables

This is the final section of the pyramid. I had thought about leaving this section out altogether since you will probably not reach this point until fifteen years after you start the program. However, I want to finish the pyramid and show you how your complete financial plan will look in the future. To reach this point, you need to excel in both your financial planning and your career. This is the time that you will reach your peak earnings. For most people, this signifies that they will have to begin putting more and more money into their retirement accounts so that they can maintain a style of living into retirement. You started saving ten to fifteen years earlier, so your retirement is pretty much set for you, and you can now play with your money. Here you can go as risky with these investments as you want. This is money for you to pursue the things you enjoy. I have seen people use this money to purchase a cattle ranch, antique cars, guns, motorcycles, real estate, and even play poker. You are at the point in your life that you can go for some really big gains because you can afford to take the risks. In addition, you now have the money to pursue the things in life you enjoy without having to worry about how you will fund your retirement or send your kids to school or buy a new car. So here is what the complete financial pyramid looks like.

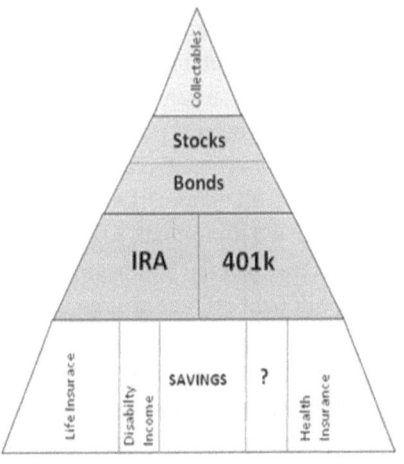

Hopefully now you can see why they call it financial planning. The majority of this pyramid is planning ahead. Sections 1 to 3 are all planning for the future and how to avoid credit card debt that will keep you from reaching the next level. It takes a significant amount of discipline to actually build this pyramid, and unfortunately, most people do not. It requires that you forgo a new car when you graduate college, and you may have to live in a small apartment or townhome a little longer than your friends, but believe me once you reach section 4, it will all be worth it. You can live a lifestyle that is ten times better than anyone in your peer group and still sleep better because you do not have to worry about losing your job or credit card companies raising your monthly payments and, most importantly, how you will support yourself in retirement.

HOW TO BEGIN

When I started writing this book, my hope was that it reaches people at a young-enough age that I can prevent them from piling on too much debt. That is why I started right in on how to begin building the financial pyramid. So if you are one of these lucky persons, then this chapter will serve as a reminder to you of why you want to avoid credit card debt. For everyone else, you probably saw the illustrations and the numbers and said, "Wow, but I could never afford to do that with my bills." Well, this section is for you.

If you do have high credit card debt, your number 1 priority is to eliminate that. You cannot reach your financial goals with high credit card debt; you are just wasting money on interest. To do this, your life will probably become really difficult; as I said before, discipline is the key. You need to set up a budget and see what it is that you are spending the majority of your money on. It might mean that you have to cut back and eat at home every night; whatever it is, it will probably hurt a little bit. The next thing is to see if you can eliminate some debts. If you just bought a brand-new vehicle and the payments are too high, trade it in for something that's older and runs good. If you bought a huge sixty-inch flat-screen plasma TV, see if you can sell it and pay off the debt. Look for your extravagant purchases and see if there is a way to lower your debt. Hopefully, this will allow you to free up enough money.

Now every dime you have extra will go into paying off debt. Start with the smallest bill you have and put as much extra as you can on it. Once this one is paid off, you will go to the next smallest. For this one, you will put the money you had budgeted for the bill you just paid off plus the extra money you found in your budget. Here is an example: Assume that you have two bills and $100 leftover. One bill is $1,000 with a $20-a-month payment. The other is $1,500 with a $30-a-month payment. So you will begin with the $1,000 bill since it is the lowest and pay the $20 payment plus the $100 you have left over. As soon as you have that bill paid off, you will go to the $1,500 bill. You can now pay the $30 payment, plus the $20 you have now that the other bill is paid off, plus the $100 you had left over. This means you will have $150 to pay toward the bill.

Continue paying off your bills like this, until all your credit card debt is gone. Once more, I define credit card debt as unnecessary or unplanned debt. This should free up enough money that you can begin working on section 1 of the pyramid. If you find that you cannot cut back and eliminate debt enough to have any extra to pay in, then your only alternative is to find more income. This may mean a weekend job or one in the afternoons. It will not be a fun time, but you can never build your financial pyramid with credit card debt. So you need to buckle down and eliminate that debt. I wish I could give you a magic formula that would cause the credit card companies to just wipe off thousands of dollars of debt, but that is not going to happen.

You need to begin building your emergency savings plan as soon as you have enough money freed up to begin saving. I would not recommend paying off all debt before you start, just enough to free up money for savings. The reason for this is that without your emergency savings set up, you are running the risk of taking on more debt. If you have money put away, when something comes up, you can cover it without adding to the debt that you are working so hard to pay off. However, you cannot move to section 2 until you have the credit card debt paid off.

Home Mortgage

Earlier in the book I talked about using debt to leverage your home. Now I want to talk more about home mortgages. Investors from all over the world saw what can happen when the public is uneducated about financial instruments. Beginning in the last quarter of 2008 into 2009, banks made a huge mess that you had to deal with called subprime mortgages. What it all boiled down to is that people were getting loans that they never should. Therefore, I think that it is important to take some time and educate you on home mortgages.

Fixed and ARMS

The two main categories are fixed rate mortgages and ARMs. ARM stands for adjustable rate mortgage. So you can probably summarize that the fixed-rate mortgages means you have a rate that is held constant for the duration of the loan. Two most common are thirty-year and fifteen-year fixed mortgages. For these loans, you and the loan officer determine the market rate for the loan and the duration. From that, the loan officer tells you that you will have to pay a certain amount of money every month for fifteen or thirty years. As I am sure you can imagine the payments for a thirty-year loan are much lower than the payments for a fifteen-year loan.

The second option is an ARM. The rate of interest on an ARM changes at set intervals—some are every quarter, every year, etc. Some of the interest rates are based on an average of the past rates for the year; some are the going interest rate plus a small percentage. There are many different types of ARMs available. All of these variables are determined when you meet with the loan officer. Unlike the fixed mortgages, you do not have a set payment to make for fifteen or thirty years because your payment changes based on what the market does. There are times when ARMs are very good, times such as the 1970s when interest rates were extremely high and then began falling steadily.

If you do not have a PhD in economics, I would never recommend that you purchase your home with an ARM. The reason for this is that the basic premise behind an ARM is that you pay interest only. This makes the payment extremely cheap every month. All you are paying is the interest on your loan and never paying anything on the loan. If this is the loan you have for your home, you will never own your home. You are simply renting the home from the bank. The ARM is an investment loan. An example is remodeling Victorian homes to resale. If you buy the Victorian home to remodel it and then resale, it is an investment to you. You are hoping to turn a profit on the home, and you do not care about owning the home. In this case you would take out an ARM on the house, pay the interest only each month and hope that you can remodel the home and sell it for more that what you have paid.

Your home, however, should not be treated as an investment property. For an investment to have a return, there needs to be a certain amount of risk that the investor takes. This idea of investment risk is that you may lose all the money you invested, and when it comes to your home, your equity in the house is a secondary concern. The first concern is what your family will do if you lose your primary residence. For this reason, I recommend a fifteen—or thirty-year fixed rate mortgage. A fifteen-year mortgage is ideal; however, with the price of homes today, the payments on a fifteen-year mortgage are usually way outside of most people's budget.

PAYING YOUR HOME OFF EARLY

There are two primary arguments about paying your mortgage off early. The first says that you should not pay extra on your home mortgage because it is a bad investment. The other argument is that the security and money you save in interest makes paying off your home early a wonderful investment. Both arguments make valid points; however, it is a great idea to pay your home off early because the savings from not paying interest will save you thousands of dollars over the life of the loan.

INTEREST

When you invest money, the bank or mutual fund is borrowing the money from you. To compensate you for letting them use the money, they pay you interest. When you borrow money from the bank, it works the same way. You get the money, and to compensate the bank, you pay it interest. So when you are receiving interest, you want to maximize your time in the market; the opposite is true when you are paying interest—you want to minimize your time in the market.

Take a look at an example. If you buy a home for $200,000 with a thirty-year mortgage at 7% interest, your monthly payment will be $1,330.60. Over the course of the year, you will pay $15,967.26. Of that $15,967.26, approximately $13,935.64 will go to interest alone. This leaves $2,031.62 to go toward the principal of your loan. Here is a table that shows the amortization of the loan over ten years.

Year	Total Payments	Total Interest	Principal Reduction for the Year
1	$15,967.26	$13,935.64	$2,031.62
2	$15,967.26	$13,788.77	$2,178.49
3	$15,967.26	$13,631.29	$2,335.97
4	$15,967.26	$13,462.42	$2,504.84
5	$15,967.26	$13,281.35	$2,685.91
6	$15,967.26	$13,087.18	$2,880.08
7	$15,967.26	$12,878.98	$3,088.28
8	$15,967.26	$12,655.73	$3,311.53
9	$15,967.26	$12,416.34	$3,550.92
10	$15,967.26	$12,159.65	$3,807.61

As you can see, the payments you make each month does not change, and over the course of a year, you will pay in $15,967.26. The majority of your payments for the first ten years go toward interest, and in fact, it is not until after year 20 that you reach a point where more of the payment is going to reduce the principal of the loan than goes for interest. The reason for this is that the interest each month is calculated on the total balance of the loan. Since a little bit of each payment is going to pay off of the principal of the loan, the total amount decreases slightly with each payment. With the loan amount decreasing each month, the amount of interest you have to pay decreases each month, allowing more to go to principal. That is the reason why only $2,031.62 goes toward the principal in the first year, and it increases to $3,807.61 by year 10. The loan is really paid off in the last ten years; it just takes the first twenty to decrease the loan amount enough that your payments can actually pay off the loan.

To pay your home off early, you need to reduce the total loan amount as quickly as possible. By decreasing the loan amount, you will decrease the interest, which allows more and more of your payment to go toward the total loan amount. This creates a circle that accelerates the decrease in your loan amount. If you were to pay an extra $100 with your first payment and then never pay any extra again, it will cut $806.94 off your total loan. So any extra you can pay, especially upfront, decreases your loan amount exponentially. Here is a table of the above loan, but with an extra payment of $100 each month applied to the total loan balance.

Year	Total Payments	Total Interest	Principal Reduction for the Year
1	$17,167.26	$13,896.38	$3,270.88
2	$17,167.26	$13,659.93	$3,507.33
3	$17,167.26	$13,406.38	$3,760.88
4	$17,167.26	$13,134.51	$4,032.75
5	$17,167.26	$12,842.98	$4,324.28
6	$17,167.26	$12,530.38	$4,636.88
7	$17,167.26	$12,195.18	$4,972.08
8	$17,167.26	$11,835.75	$5,331.51
9	$17,167.26	$11,450.33	$5,716.93
10	$17,167.26	$11,037.06	$6,130.20

In this table, the principal reduction each year is growing much more rapidly than in the other table. Take a look at the difference in year 10. The total payments are up to $17,167.26, which is $1,200 more than the first table. However, the principal reduction in year 10 is $6,130.20, which is $2,322.59 more than the first table. By paying the extra $100 a month, you have successfully decreased the total loan amount, thereby decreasing your interest expense by $1,122.59 for the year.

At this current rate, you will pay off the loan in twenty-four years and three months. However, it does more than just pay off the loan faster. Because interest is accrued each month off of the total loan amount, you are saving money every month by paying extra. The extra money decreases the total loan amount and thereby decreases the amount of interest you have to pay. This means more of your payment goes toward paying off your loan instead of as interest. If you were to make the minimum payment of $1,330.60 for thirty years, you would pay in $479,017.80. So your $200,000 loan ends up costing you $479,017.80, and $279,017.80 of that is simply interest you pay to the bank. By paying an extra $100 each month, you decrease your total payout to $415,704.33, and you have just saved $63,313.47 in interest that you will not have to pay to the bank.

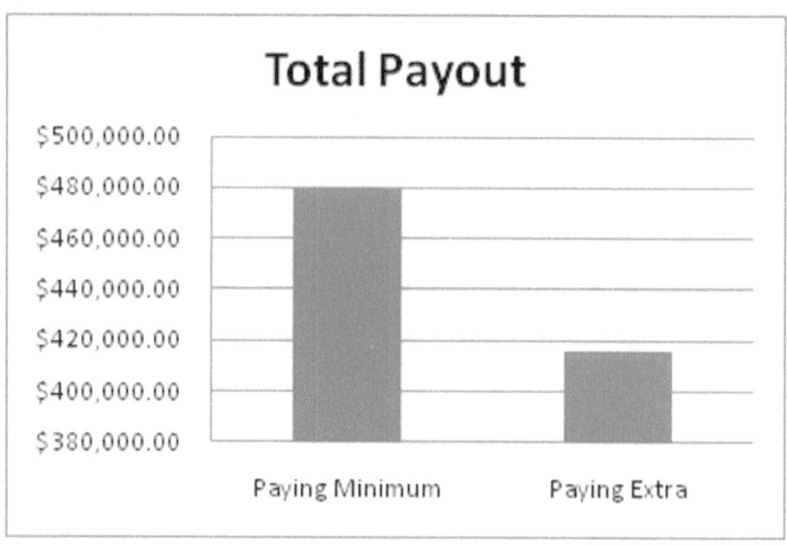

Total Payout

$500,000.00	
$480,000.00	
$460,000.00	
$440,000.00	
$420,000.00	
$400,000.00	
$380,000.00	
Paying Minimum	Paying Extra

Any amount that you can pay extra, especially at the beginning of the loan, will save you large amounts of money over the life of the loan. People will argue that your home is not a good investment, and therefore, any extra money should be put into other investments instead of paying off your home. When you just look at it, this seems to make sense; any equity you have in your home is illiquid, has a low return, and is not tax advantageous. However, you need to look at it from a different angle. You have to have a place to live, so why not pay as little for that as you can. I have already shown that by paying an extra $100 a month, you will drastically cut the expense of your home. So if you think about your loan, it is money that you have to pay. There is no way around it, or else you will be living out on the street. Therefore, any way that you can save money on that will be a gain to you. So by "investing" $29,100 extra ($100 for twenty-four years and three months) in your home, you will have a return of $63,313.47 or a 118% return over that time period. In addition, think about how much income you would actually need in retirement if you did not have to worry about a mortgage payment.

The Dream

This book is not intended to be an investment guide. There is no place in here that I try and tell you which stocks to pick or what trading software to buy. In fact, I tend to discourage you from trying that. What my intention is for this book is to help you obtain a dream. I want to motivate you to set financial goals for your life, and then help you establish a path that will make these dreams a reality.

Reaching your financial dreams will not be easy. It takes a lot of hard work to follow the plan that I laid out in this book. You must learn to discipline yourself. However, I can promise you that every sacrifice you make right now will pay off in the future. I am imploring you to not try and keep up with your peers. If they want to max out credit cards and buy new toys on debt, do not follow after them. By building financial stability, you will one day have the financial means to purchase double of everything your friends have, but with cash. You will have a better life without the stress that debt brings along.

Dreams are almost never easy to obtain. Men have poured their whole lives into their dreams because they felt it was worth every sacrifice. I hope that, after reading this book, you can now establish some financial goals for your life. I can give you goals for your life, but if you are not willing to buy into them, they will never materialize. It is very difficult for us to make sacrifices for someone else's dream. That is why I am encouraging you to set down and create goals for yourself, and they need to be goals that are big enough to keep you on track when you do not want to stick to a budget. It has to be a dream that will keep you looking toward the future, and it will allow you to take advantage of opportunities along the way. "If one does not know to which port one is sailing, no wind is favorable."